I Could Have Been
a Cabdriver...
But I Became
an Actor Instead

Published by
Smith and Kraus, Inc.
177 Lyme Road, Hanover, NH 03755
www.SmithKraus.com

Cover and Text Design by Freedom Hill Design, Reading, Vermont
Front cover photos by Leroy Koetz

First edition: April 2002
9 8 7 6 5 4 3 2 1

Library of Congress Cataloging In Publication Information

Cerny, JoBe.
I could have been a cabdriver...but I became an actor instead : a practical
guide to the business of professional acting / JoBe Cerny. —1st ed.
p. cm. — (Career development series)
ISBN 1-57525-302-X
1. Acting-Vocational guidance. I. Title. II. Series.

PN2055 .C38 2002
792'.028'023—dc21
2002276540

I Could Have Been a Cabdriver...

But I Became an Actor Instead

A Practical Guide
to the Business
of Professional Acting

JoBe Cerny

CAREER DEVELOPMENT SERIES

A Smith and Kraus Book

In Memory of
Doctor Fred Sitton

AUTHOR'S ACKNOWLEDGMENTS

I would like to thank Leroy Koetz for the cover photography, and Robert Brooks and the Proctor & Gamble Corporation for allowing me to use the pictures. I would like to thank Professor Richard Pick and Dr. John Paul of Valparaiso University for giving me the opportunity to share my experiences with their students, and Barbara Robertson of Columbia College for suggesting I put my lectures into book form. I would also like to thank my editor, Evelyn Chen, who was such a pleasure to work with.

Contents

Please note the actual title of each chapter is listed for people with a sense of humor.
An alternate business title is listed in parenthesis for the more serious among us.

PART TWO
Business and Art

FOREWORD

Who is JoBe Cerny?

JoBe Cerny has been a professional actor for the past thirty-two years. He has consistently been in the top 2 percent of wage earners in Screen Actor's Guild for the past two decades. JoBe is best known as the voice of the Pillsbury Doughboy, and, on camera, as Proctor & Gamble's silent spokesman for Cheer Detergent. His work has won nearly every major award in advertising including the Golden Lion at the Cannes International Film Festival for the best commercial in the world. *Ad Age, EntertainmentWeekly, T.V. Guide,* and Nickelodeon have all rated his work among the fifty greatest commercials of all time. On stage, he has performed in thirty-five plays and worked extensively in improvisational theater. He toured nationally for *The Second City.* He has also appeared in many feature films and numerous television shows. Additionally, he has performed in 2,500 commercials. He has performed in hundreds of videos, most notably in star-ring roles for John Cleese's Video Arts. JoBe is also a well respected member of AFTRA, SAG, and Actor's Equity and is involved with developing union contracts for new technology.

In addition to his acting work, JoBe has had a twenty-five-year career as a writer, director, and producer. His Chicago production company, Cerny/American Creative, is nationally recognized for excellence in sound design. JoBe designed and built the first digitally networked recording studios in the United States. His company currently produces 400 projects annually covering a range of work from commercials, music, and industrial videos to feature films. His company recently produced its 5,500th consecutive project without going over-budget on a single project. JoBe is a recommended speaker of the American Advertising Federation on the subject of creativity. He also is a regular speaker on the college circuit on the Business of Acting.

WHO SHOULD READ THIS BOOK?

This book is written for anyone who is interested in the profession of acting. That group would include students, working professional actors, and amateur actors who wish to turn a hobby into a profession. But, this book has a broader appeal than just a textbook for actors. This book gives a fascinating behind-the-scenes look at what it really takes to be an actor. So, its base of readers would also include people who like to read about actors and how they got to be actors. Theatrical writers, directors, producers, and agents have also found this book both informative and useful. Because of Mr. Cerny's success in commercials, people involved with advertising are very interested in a behind-the-scenes look at the man behind the Pillsbury Doughboy and the the Cheer Man.

WHAT CAN SOMEONE EXPECT FROM THIS BOOK?

This book was developed from thirty years of practical experience and twenty-five years of workshops and question & answer sessions at universities with aspiring actors. This is not a primer book; many other books exist that explain how to write résumés, get head shots, find agents, and all the basics of how to get into the business of acting. This book explains how to stay in the business of acting. This book answers questions that keep actors up nights. As the subtitle implies, it is a practical guide to the *business* of professional acting. This book asks and answers the hard questions. It is a real gut check.

These chapters are based on lectures that have helped many students go onto full-time careers as actors. The business approach used in this book has been proven successful. However, these chapters also paint a very realistic picture of the level of commitment it takes to succeed as an actor. Not everyone has what it takes. Some students have changed focus after the dose of reality this book offers. In any case, the book is an advanced one that will inspire introspection.

One last word, Mr. Cerny has been a professional comedian his entire life. The reader of this book can expect to laugh and be entertained — from cover to cover.

Smith and Kraus Publishers

PART ONE

THE BUSINESS
OF ACTING

Many people want to be professional actors but few ever attain that status. The thing that separates professional actors from the rest is their ability to successfully manage the business aspects of their acting careers. To become a professional in any occupation means that a person is proficient at their craft and will derive a livable income from their work. While many actors are trained to act, few are taught how to make money from the practice of their craft. This section explains how professional actors make money and manage to make acting a full-time occupation.

I Could Have Been a Cabdriver...

(Making a Career Choice)

I could have been a cabdriver. In fact, I could have become a cabdriver during perhaps the last "Golden Age" of cabdrivers. You see, once upon a time, there was a company that made cars that were designed to be cabs. They were called Checkers. They weren't family sedans converted to taxicab use. They were designed to be cabs. They had huge rear seats that made them easy to get into and out of. They were made for short trips. They stood out from every other car on the street. They were special. They were cabs. Streets of major cities had thousands of them coming from every direction. To get one to take you somewhere, all you had to do was hold up your hand on any street corner and dozens of them would descend upon you.

The thing I find really amazing is that Checker Cabs were made in Kalamazoo, Michigan. Usually, necessity is the mother of invention. Somehow, I can't imagine needing enough cabs in Kalamazoo to build a cab factory there. In fact, I bet a cab would be a rare commodity in Kalamazoo, even during rush hour. It would seem that New York or Chicago would be a logical place to find a cab factory since they have cabs everywhere in those places. You wouldn't have to ship the cabs from Kalamazoo; they'd just be there. But, maybe that is too logical. And, some things are just meant to be wondrous — like cab companies in Kalamazoo and me actually becoming a professional actor.

To understand all this, maybe I better go back a few years to the formative years of my career. I had been a professional actor for about two and a half years when I decided working in a Repertory Company and doing twenty-six plays wasn't enough. I decided to set my sights higher and enrolled in the Northwestern University Theater Department to get an advanced degree. The twenty-six plays made me aware of various personal shortcomings, and I thought graduate school would be the perfect place to hone my craft — and like so many of my classmates, I thought: "With a master's, I can always teach!" I completed my course work in a year, passed my comprehensives and received a M.A. of theater from Northwestern University in 1972. I felt smarter and more confident in my craft, but the crowning piece of education was still to come. I had been waiting several weeks for an appointment to see the head of the Northwestern Theater Department to ask him the answer to the BIG QUESTION, the Holy Grail all actors eternally seek.

I was nervous as I awaited his arrival. In my heart, I knew if he could just answer one simple question for me, I'd live a happier life. I'd be at peace with my future. The knot in my stomach would be gone and my education would be complete. He burst into the room looking very busy, acting very busy, and in fact informed me that he was "very busy." He had to review the final scene from *Romeo & Juliet* so he could help some of his acting students work through the scene. I wondered why a Ph.D. of theater needed to review this scene. I thought about offering him some help, but he seemed so busy. "So what did you want to see me about," he asked? This was going to be the big moment. I was about to gain the missing link that would synergize my entire education. I asked the question that puzzles every actor the most: "How do I go about getting into the business?" There was a moment of silence before he laughed. "Is that what you wanted to see me about? I don't know. I suppose you go out and get a job driving a cab and then maybe you'll get a beer commercial some day." He then slapped me on the back and wished me luck. Five years of college culminated in that one encounter. The head of the theater department of one of the most prestigious theater schools in the country had no idea how to get into the business he was training people to enter. If I had listened to him, I might be a cabdriver today. . . but, I became an actor instead. So, take heart.

After that fateful meeting, I promised myself that if I ever became successful as an actor, I would go back to universities and try to help budding actors find an answer to that question. This book contains my thoughts over the past three decades about this difficult question. I frequently speak to actors at universities. I cannot tell you how many seniors raise their trembling hands and, with a look of fear in their eyes, say: "I'm going to graduate in two weeks. I'm going to get a degree in theater. My parents spent a fortune on my education. What do I do now??? I don't have the vaguest idea."

I usually take a moment of silence (for dramatic effect), give them a little laugh, slap them on the back, and say: "When I graduated with a master's of theater from Northwestern, I decided to become a cabdriver. I wanted to become a cabdriver more than anything else in the world. But every other theater major in the city got there before I did and no cab-driving jobs were available to me. I considered waiting tables as a second choice. Again, most of those jobs were filled by theater majors. So, I decided to start spending my days and nights looking for acting work, and I became a professional actor instead." Here's how I went about it.

CHAPTER TWO

I Could Have Been a Teacher...

(Education)

After reading the first chapter, some people might think I'm presenting a pretty negative picture of the Northwestern University theater department. I'm not. I'm presenting a realistic picture of how most university people view the acting profession. Even for most actors in the business, the profession of acting is a crapshoot. There is no rhyme or reason as to why one person succeeds and another fails. Legend has it that Lana Turner was discovered having a soda in a drugstore. It seems almost all actors have been cabdrivers or waiters at one time or another. So, the myth perpetuates itself. Get a menial job and wait for your big break. Unfortunately, if you do that, your odds of success over the long term are very long odds indeed. You'll get good at menial labor instead of acting.

A university's primary goal is to teach you how to study acting. Except for a few professional acting schools, universities don't even train you to become an actor. A college education in theater gives you a basic education to begin your career as an artist. This is something most actors have a difficult time understanding. When you complete a degree, your mind-set is that you have finished training. The reality of the matter is that you are minimally qualified to begin training.

As I neared graduation, I attended a seminar in which the speaker told the assembled acting students who were eager to embark upon their careers that the odds of any person in the room ever becoming a professional actor were almost zero. Of the over one hundred students present, he predicted only two of us would have careers. As I looked out over the crowd, my only thought was: "I wonder who the other person is?" I'll talk more about postive mental attitude and confidence in one's ability later, but, at that moment, I can't tell you how angry I felt, and how determined I was to prove him wrong. Unfortunately, he was 100 percent correct. Statistics support his statement. Each year, universities graduate thousands of theater students. The actual job openings for these people are very few and far between, and they become the largest age group of actors entering the profession. It is a classic case of supply and demand. There is a glut of twenty year olds entering the market and going into competition for a limited supply of work. Additionally, there is a large group of professional actors who didn't go to college and have several years of experience under their belts competing for the same roles. There are currently about 135,000 actors in the acting unions. About 10 percent of them earn full-time livings as actors. Also competing for the same work are countless nonunion actors who are willing to work for less money. The actor graduating from college goes to the end of the line behind all these actors.

This is the point at which a lot of actors become overwhelmed. The idea of driving a cab or waiting tables seems like a safe approach to a tenuous future. Or, in many cases, graduates think: "Hey, I've got a degree! I can teach!" Teaching jobs pay far better than cab-driving jobs, but you need to be fair to yourself. Do you really want to teach? I cannot tell you how many people I know who wanted to be actors ended up teaching because it was a safer path. Some of those people became great teachers, but many of them felt unfulfilled. They felt they could have succeeded if someone had just given them a chance, or if they had been in the right place at the right time, or if they had been better connected. And so, now they teach what they studied while they were in school instead of what they did while they practiced the craft of acting. They teach from research instead of from experience.

I considered teaching after I got my B.A. in Speech and Drama from Valparaiso University. In fact, I was offered a very good job teaching at Chesterton High School in Chesterton, Indiana. Because I had been a professional theater actor for two years, the school thought I would bring a lot to the position. The salary I was offered for teaching was a lot more than I was getting for acting in the theater full-time. I'd get health insurance. I'd get a chance to direct. In a year or two, I'd have a house, a new car, and a safe predictable future. Life would be mapped out for me. There wouldn't be the uncertainty and risk associated with an acting career.

This is the point at which a lot of actors give in to reality. Something is better than maybe-something. It's not major motion pictures or Broadway, but at least it's real instead of a dream. When I was offered the teaching job, I told myself that I would grow to love it. I loved kids, I loved school. Why not? I was ready to sign my teaching contract, when my Lana Turner moment happened.

CHAPTER THREE

I Could Have Been Lana Turner...
(Employment Opportunities)

When a million-to-one shot comes through, it is great theater. A small-town girl orders a soda at a drugstore counter and a big producer discovers her and makes her into a big Hollywood star. Audiences loved it. Rocky Balboa, a nobody from Palookaville, gets a shot at the World Heavyweight Championship and wins! The crowd goes wild. I'm ready to sign a teaching contract to make me a role model for *Mr. Holland's Opus II*, when I get an unexpected letter in the mail. I'll never forget those fateful words:

"Dear Mr. Cerny, We know a lot about you. We know who you are and where you live. Doesn't sound like much? Well, we also know you are going to be drafted very soon. Why not come in and see us?" The letter was signed by the local armed forces recruiter. There was a conflict in Vietnam. Teaching deferments were no longer going to be granted. My safe future was gone and I was going to be a soldier — a job that actually paid less money than I earned as a theater actor. But, at that moment, fate played a key role in my acting career. If I had signed that contract, I'd probably be teaching somewhere right now. If I had signed that contract, I would have been comfortable and safe, and I would have never had to try to defy the odds. I would never have forced myself to take the difficult path instead of the easy one.

In retrospect, I don't think I really wanted to teach. I wanted to live a more comfortable life. When I was with the Repertory Company, things were great. I didn't need to look for work; it was always there for me. Or, so I thought. One night, between shows, I was talking to our stage manager, Casey. Casey was in his sixties and had been in the business for years. I asked him what it was like having a career that lasted almost forty years. He said that after forty years he was no different than me. He never knew where his next job or next dime was coming from. He said if the theater closed tomorrow, he'd be out of work with no prospects. That comment hit me like a bag of cement. I was young and hadn't reached a very high standard of living yet. I was doing just fine; I was acting and eating. I had a one-room trailer. What more could I want? But then, for a brief moment, I put myself in Casey's shoes. I knew I didn't want to find myself in those shoes forty years later. Teaching looked good. Graduate school looked good. But, the army came first.

CHAPTER FOUR

I Could Have Been a Soldier...

(Career Satisfaction)

Have you ever worked with a director who wanted everything done exactly the way he does it? That was what the army was like. The army was not a creative environment — and, quite frankly, the costumes weren't the best. It took me less than a day to realize that I was not going to be a career soldier. When our sergeant addressed us as "the mens," I knew this was not the place for me. The good news was that I had a lot of time on my hands since my main job seemed to be guarding Louisiana from Mississippi. I had lots of time to think. I could guard and think although the sergeant never allowed "the mens" to march and chew gum.

Actually, I had a lot to think about. I had a college degree in speech and drama, two years of professional theater experience, a teaching offer, and an offer for a teaching assistantship for Northwestern Graduate School. Not bad for a guy stuck in a $90 a month job. I really liked acting, but could I deal with the uncertainty of never knowing when or where the next job was coming from? Casey's dose of reality made me think. The other actors in the Repertory Company made me think, too. Many of them went to professional schools instead of universities. I was trained to think; they were trained to act. So, I decided to think about what made me different from them. The big difference was physical training. The hours I spent in literature and theater history courses, they spent in dance classes, voice classes, and stage combat classes. I needed to become a better actor to remain competitive, so I decided to accept the graduate school offer at Northwestern. Since you already know that Northwestern Graduate School pointed me in the direction of a cab-driving career, let me tell you what I learned about acting in the army. It's a lesson that convinced me that it was worth giving up a predictable future to take the risk I needed to take to become a professional actor.

I was in the army during the Vietnam conflict. The government had trouble attracting enough volunteers. A lot of people were drafted, but the army likes volunteers. Since the jail system was overflowing, certain offenders were given the option of volunteering for the army instead of serving jail sentences. After I finished my tour of guarding Louisiana from Mississippi, I was transferred to Oklahoma and assigned to a new company to begin the study of tanks. We arrived at our new barracks around midnight. Our new sergeant welcomed all us new "mens." He made a special point to single out two of the new "mens" that were joining the unit; it was his obligation to inform us that one of them was a convicted rapist and the other a convicted murderer. Both had volunteered for the army to gain early release from jail. The sergeant then told us to turn the lights off in ten minutes and have a pleasant night's rest.

What has this got to do with acting????? Believe it or not, these two guys, the rapist and the murderer, became the first two fans I ever had. Many actors become actors because they like attention. Once these two guys discovered that I was an actor, they were in awe of me. They had never met an actor. In civilian life, other guys in the unit were mechanics, plumbers, car dealers, landscapers, accountants, rapists, and murderers. But I was the only actor. To them, I was special. They wanted to hear everything about it. Much to their credit, they never asked me to perform "Plant a Radish" from *The Fantasticks!* And thank God, they never asked me to dance "The Rape Ballet" from the same show. They used to like to hang around with me, look at me, and listen to me. (And when you come right down to it, isn't that what acting is all about?) Everywhere we went, they would tell people that I was an actor. Drill sergeants would say: "Really? Wow, that's neat!" Sure, this sounds very bizarre, but it taught me something that I'll always appreciate. Acting is a very special job. Just about everyone thinks it's glamorous and neat. If you ever actually get to be a professional actor, it is something you'll be proud of for the rest of your life. I can't tell you what it felt like the first time I saw my name on the door of my trailer on a movie I did for Twentieth Century Fox. I can't tell you how thrilled I was to see myself on a movie theater screen for the first time. And, when I got my first above the line starring role in a play and saw my name in lights on the theater marquee, I nearly cried. How many people have thrills like this in a lifetime? The life of an actor is a charmed existence that makes the struggle well worth the effort. People notice you — they want to get to know you and shake your hand. When I was acting at The Second City earning $150 a week, a teenage stock boy followed me around the grocery store trying to build up the courage to ask me for an autograph. My friends who were working as waiters were making more money in tips than I was, but no one was asking them for their autographs. When I was in the army, it wasn't like I was Bob Hope or Brooke

Shields visiting the troops, but it was nice getting to know my "fans," even though one was a rapist and one was a murderer. The very fact that I was a professional actor brought something special to their lives. It was nice being appreciated, and it gave my ego the important boost it needed for the next step in my career.

CHAPTER FIVE

I Could Have Been a Golf Pro...
(Career Planning)

My parents never dreamed I'd become an actor. They wanted me to become a golf pro. They somehow thought that would be a nice, secure life. As I started to play in amateur tournaments, I quickly learned that a one-foot putt could cause more anxiety than any opening night. Some types of pressure make you rise to the occasion and other types make you crazy. I emoted better than I putted. So now I only play golf when I want to get irritated. For me the uncertainties of being a golf pro were far scarier than the uncertainties of being an actor. I went to school to study acting — not golf. Knowledge increases confidence. I felt confident I could handle any acting problems that came my way, just like a plumber can handle any water leaks that squirt his way. But, herein lies the rub: How does a beginning actor get acting problems to leak into his life? How do you open the floodgates?

Let's go back to the cab-driver idea. If you hang around cabdrivers, you find cab-driving work; if you hang around waiters, you get waiter work; if you hang around actors, you get acting work. So, what do you do, get a map of the star's homes? Well, any good adventure begins with a map, and any worthwhile career begins with a business plan. Try to imagine where you'd like to be a year from now, five years from now, twenty-five years from now. It's a fantasy, so imagine to your heart's desire. You'll probably fall a little short of your goal, so make your fantasy a good one. This is one of the few instances in which I encourage young actors not to worry about being practical. The higher you set your goals, the harder you'll expect to work to attain them. The hardships you'll experience on the road to achieving your goals will impose practicality on you. Cabdrivers learn certain roads are easier on their cabs than others. When I first started my career, I wanted to be a comedy movie star. During my career, I've performed in over 3,000 comedy commercials, won many awards, and made a full-time living as an actor. Even though I haven't achieved my original goal, I've done a lot better than if I had set a lower goal. I certainly did better than the theater department head at Northwestern anticipated; he wished me luck hoping I'd get a beer commercial someday. I've probably done twenty or thirty of them. So, what I'm recommending is to map out a future for yourself that has a worthwhile end destination. The reason most actors' careers fail is that they don't have a plan beyond "I'll get a job driving a cab or waiting tables and see what happens." *What happens is what you make happen.* Producers, agents, and casting people are always looking for actors—but they look for them in certain places.

I think almost every little kid has had this experience at one time or another. The little kid sees the big kids playing ball and asks: "Can I play, too?" The big kids laugh and say: "Go away kid, you're bothering us." The kid comes back every day and asks the same question and gets the same answer until one day. . . one of the big kids doesn't show up to play and they need one more player. The new kid gets a chance. (If you're an actor, you find the missing actor is out playing golf.) I truly believe if you hang around the block long enough, eventually, somebody will give you a chance. Whether or not your career moves forward depends on what you do with that chance, but that's another chapter.

The big question now becomes: Where is this block where everybody is looking for actors? It can be just about anywhere. It all depends on what you really want to do. Your career must be centered in a place that has a hub of activity. Obvious locations are Hollywood and Broadway. But they could be just about anywhere. Nashville is a mecca for music. Las Vegas is a great place for dancers. Chicago is an important center for voice-over work. A lot of young actors cut their teeth in Orlando at places like Disney World. My career began in a theater in Valparaiso, Indiana. The famous Steppenwolfe Theatre Company started in a church basement in Highland Park, Illinois. One of my favorite comedy writers at The Second City, Doug Steckler, began his career in North Dakota doing stand-up in local clubs and bars.

You need to pick a place that will give you an opportunity to achieve your dream. If you live in Detroit, Michigan, it is very unlikely you will get regular opportunities to audition for Broadway plays or major motion pictures. You will get opportunities that the Detroit acting scene offers: local plays, television and radio commercials, industrial videos, and local television. Detroit is a great place to gain practical experience; but the odds of spending a forty-year career there and becoming an international star are very long indeed. But, you have to start somewhere, so pick someplace that makes sense for you. Pick a block that has the kind of action you're looking for. Once you've done that, now the real job of acting begins.

CHAPTER SIX

I Could Have Been a Door-to-Door Salesman...
(Sales)

While I was in graduate school, I needed to make money. So, I checked out the help-wanted ads. By the time I read the third ad, I knew I had found the perfect job for a busy graduate student.

> HELP WANTED
> Make your own hours.
> Be your own Boss.
> Excellent Pay for Motivated Individuals.

I was motivated, I wanted excellent pay, I wanted flexible hours, and, most of all, I wanted a boss just like me. But, what could this mystery job from heaven be? This just had to be too good to be true. Nothing this perfect ever just fell into someone's lap. But, then again, as I learned in the army, I was "special"; stuff like this just happens to actors. Well, I called the phone number and before I knew it, I was a Fuller Brush man. That's right, a door-to-door salesman just like you see in the movies. As a matter of fact, Red Skelton, one of my favorite comedians, played a Fuller Brush man in a movie called: *The Fuller Brush Man.* Maybe this was a sign that I'd get a leading role in the near future.

Being an actor, I knew I could play this part. For customers to believe that I was a brush man, I knew I had to look like a brush man. So, I dressed the part. I had a conservative sport coat from High School that matched my sample case. To be successful at this, I knew I needed the right look. So, I got shirts and ties from Sears because they created an image that said I was hardworking and respectable but needy enough that people would feel sorry for me and buy something from me. I was given a territory near campus; and in between classes, motivated and confident, I hit the street.

Being a door-to-door salesperson is an experience every actor should have. This type of work is far more valuable than cabdriving or waiting on tables could ever be. It teaches you that "Necessity is the mother of invention." As I mentioned, I was motivated and confident, I dressed the part, and I was ready to act the part. Every good comedy actor knows that no matter how hard you rehearse you never know where all the laughs will come until the audience tells you. My first day was a real eye-opener. I'd ring a doorbell and wait for somebody to answer the door. When they'd answer, I'd say: "Hi, I'm the Fuller Brush man." That line was usually enough to bring down the house. People would laugh and say: "You're kidding! Are you for real? I didn't know you guys really existed!" After a week of this, I realized that this was not going to be as easy as I thought it would be. To this day, I have a soft spot in my heart and a healthy respect for anyone who can successfully make unsolicited sales. At this point, I'd like to expose you to a very sobering thought: Every successful actor I know spends a majority of their time making unsolicited sales calls. This is especially true when you are just beginning a career. Your job is selling yourself to agents, producers, directors, writers, and creative directors.

Until you make a sale, you don't get to act. It is as simple as that. As soon as you complete an acting job, you are out of work and need to start the sales process all over again. Throughout your career, one person is responsible for finding you acting work: you. If you want to become a successful actor, you must become a successful salesperson first.

When I became a Fuller Brush man, it was winter. Chicago is very cold in the winter. Walking door-to-door, getting laughs instead of sales was a difficult thing to deal with. If I didn't get into a house to warm up every twenty to thirty minutes, I found that my nose started to run, my glasses would frost over, and my lips would get numb from the cold, making it hard to talk. I mention this because it is a feeling the beginning actor will have over and over again. That feeling will test your confidence and question your motivation. How you deal with this feeling separates the actors from the teachers. *Callous* is a word to mull over. How badly do you want to become a professional actor? Do you want it badly enough to do door-to-door sales?

As I got ready to ring my next doorbell, something wonderful happened. Two kids were playing in the front yard of their house. As the mother answered the door, one kid took a broom and broke it over the other kid's back. (They wore down jackets, so he didn't get hurt.) The kids yelled at each other, the mother yelled at the kids, and I observed. The mother shagged the kids inside while I picked up the broken broom. And then, it came to me! As I handed the mother her broken broom, I said: "Hi, I'm your Fuller Brush man. We have a special today on brooms." She invited me in, made me a cup of cocoa, bought a broom, and a whole bunch of other stuff — and just like that, I knew what I had to do to become a professional actor.

As I sipped my cocoa, I knew Stanislavski would be very proud of me. My perception of motivation and of actor needs and wants was more acute than it had ever been before because of this incident. People buy things they want or need. I found a customer with a need — the mother needed a broom. I made a sale by fulfilling that need — I was Johnny-on-the-spot with a broom. A producer needs actors. Think of an actor as a product that can fulfill a need. Find out what people are looking for and then try to convince them that you are exactly what they are looking for. The lady needed a broom, so I offered her a broom. If I had offered a hairbrush, I don't think she would have taken time to see me. Her response would have been: "I'm kind of busy, I've got to go out and buy a broom." It's hard to sell refrigerator magnets to Eskimos who don't have refrigerators. If a producer is casting for a motherly, elderly woman, don't try to sell yourself for the part if you're a short, stocky man (unless you're Nathan Lane). If you want to find work, find people who need what you do.

CHAPTER SEVEN

I Could Have Been
a Mad Scientist...
(Product Development)

Frankenstein with Boris Karloff is one of my favorite pictures. One guy builds another guy. When I was a kid, nobody in my neighborhood did that kind of stuff. I always thought it would be neat to go down in the basement and build somebody. My dad had a good wood shop in the basement. Maybe Pinocchio would have been a little more realistic as a goal. I loved the idea of being a mad scientist for an occupation. Nearly failing biology and getting average grades in woodworking threw a wet blanket over my basement Frankenstein and Pinocchio projects. But, being an actor means creating another being at one time or another in your career. The being that you create is going to be the product that fulfills the producer's needs I talked about in the last chapter.

A lot of successful actors talk about themselves as if they are talking about someone else. Their agents and producers talk about them more like they would talk about companies than about people. They become a product. "I need a Cruise or a Newman for this project" shouts the frustrated producer who can't get either of them for his project. "Get me a Cruise, a Newman, two Coca-Colas, and a Big Mac." These are all brand-name products. With a Big Mac you get two all-beef patties, special sauce, lettuce, cheese, pickles, onions on a sesame seed bun — with a Newman, you get blue eyes. You know what you're getting when you buy a brand-name product. You know what you're getting when you buy a well-known actor.

When you are starting out, you don't have a reputation or identity. You are an unknown quantity. Your picture or your name are all that can attract attention to you. Image is all an actor has. That image is a combination of looks, sound, and ability. Selling an actor is like selling perfume. There is a certain amount of substance that is enhanced by a whole lot of image. The image part is what makes you unforgettable — or extremely forgettable. Look in the mirror. Ask yourself two questions: "What do I see?" and "What do I want to see?" The first question is a question that relates to the physical; the second question is spiritual.

So, "Mirror, Mirror on the wall, who's the fairest of them all?" If the mirror says: "You look like Roseanne," deal with the hand you were dealt. You may not be the "fairest of them all," but you obviously can work all the time. Roseanne has an image countless people like to see and can identify with. Producers look for "Roseanne types" for roles. Roseanne created an image that was usable and saleable. People bought it. But, more importantly, Roseanne became the best Roseanne anyone could be. She played the hand she was dealt and enhanced it with character. I had a chance to work with Mr. T in a movie. Talk about a person who created a memorable image! Mr. T is truly one of a kind. Again, he played the hand he was dealt and made the most of it. In the scene I did with Mr. T, he gets enraged and throws me through a door. Being out of control is certainly in keeping with Mr. T's image; however, as a person, I found him to be a very professional performer who was very much in control when he created chaos. He was a very good performer to work with.

Once you come to grips with what you look like, you need to figure out where you fit in the industry. Watch movies, TV shows, commercials, and theater. See who is like you and what they do. You will get a realistic picture of who your competition is and what they are capable of doing. *Doing* is the key word. The most important part of acting is doing. Acting is a physical profession. If you can't do it physically, you can't do it. Everyone has physical limitations. Don't tell people you can do things you can't do. (Don't tell people you are a martial arts expert so you can do a fight scene with Steven Segal — unless you really know how to take a punch.) Find out what you do better than anyone else and then hone your ability.

When I was performing at The Second City in Chicago, I discovered that people liked watching me do things. Frequently, I didn't say anything in scenes. I spent my time concentrating on making my movements interesting. I gained a reputation as a physical comedian. I didn't have to talk because I was funny to watch. Frequently, people come up to me and say: "I didn't know you could talk!" This is pretty ironic since much of my career has been spent doing voice-overs in front of a microphone. Conversely, people in the recording industry often say to me: "I didn't know you worked on-camera!" The important thing to remember here is that I have established a memorable image in two very different areas of the business. People found it hard to believe that I could walk and talk. Actors who walk and talk fall into a whole different category than either of the categories I get most of my work in. It is almost like I am two completely different actors — which can work to an actor's advantage. But, that is the subject of the next chapter.

CHAPTER EIGHT

I Could Have Been Twins...
(Expanding a Product Line)

O K, you're driving your cab along the road to a successful acting career. You know where you want to end up, but, suddenly, there is a fork in the road. The more abilities you have, the more forks you get. One of the biggest mistakes the Checker Cab Company made was only making one product — cabs. Ford Motor Company makes cabs, trucks, family sedans, four-wheel drive vehicles, sports cars, convertibles, station wagons, and so on. Companies that only sold gramophones went out of business when gramophones were no longer needed. Unfortunately, many actors' careers end when they are no longer needed. They go out of style. Sometime, go back and look at old *Teen* magazines. How many five-year wonders are there in the business? How many times do you say: "Whatever happened to . . .?" When actors don't change with the times, the times often leave them behind. It is a matter of style, and style is a very fickle thing.

Tattoos and pierced body parts are very popular right now. These things have been around for centuries, but they have not received great acceptance until recently. Right now, they're hip. Twenty years ago, John Travolta's white polyester suit was hip. Walk into a club wearing that suit today and see how comfortable you feel.

Actors need to continuously evaluate their image and expand their product line. It is very difficult to be a one-trick pony. People get tired of the act. An actor's popularity ebbs and wanes over a career. If you limit your search to one type of work, there is a good chance you will hit a dry spell. When I first started my career, I knew I wanted to do movies and plays. But, when you are starting out, it is very difficult to find regular work in film and theater. Every actor wants film roles and the pickings are slim indeed for the beginner. While a beginning actor can find theater work, it is very difficult to string theater jobs back-to-back. You might do one role for six months and then not be able to line up another theater job for months. When I was doing theater, I was happy and making money, but it limited my availability to take film roles. My first movie offers were usually small parts that would result in a one- or two-day contract so I couldn't afford to give up my theater income to take them. The bottom line here is that every actor wants to do film and theater work, and there isn't enough work to keep everyone employed. The reality is that it is very difficult to make a living as an actor if you limit your search to film and theater work. No matter how talented you are you will not always be able to find jobs in film and theater. So you need to find other opportunities to earn money as an actor.

Leaving a serious acting school, your attention is focused on gaining work in theater, motion pictures, and television. However, there is something you need to know before you limit your search to this type of work. A minor portion of the money earned by all the actors in the business is made in these high-profile areas. It is true that stars makes millions doing movies and television, but there are only a few hundred actors making star money at any given time — and only a handful of those people make the big dollars for extended periods of time. How many actors star in five successful films during their entire career? The list is very short indeed.

So, actors need to know about the other ways to use their talents to make money. Ninety percent of the money earned by non-stars is made in ways you probably never dreamed of. After two years of repertory company acting and Northwestern Graduate School, I never expected to become a print model — but I did. I never dreamed that one of the forks in my road would lead me to becoming a successful producer of radio commercials, let alone the star of hundreds of industrial films. In fact, I had never heard of an industrial film until I entered the business in Chicago. There are many ways to make a living as an actor, and you need to be aware of all of them. You never know which facet of the acting business might be your niche and your source of income that allows you to have a career.

Let's start by taking a look at a career in modeling. Every actor has to have a head shot. No one will sculpt a bust of you until after you're famous, and a sculpture is a very cumbersome thing to take to auditions. So, actors need to get to know photographers. Many actors say they hate to have their pictures taken. If you are planning on getting into movies, revise your thinking; in movies they take hundreds of pictures of you all day long. Your picture is your calling card. It better be good. Many of the most famous photographers in the world have hired me as a model. Never in my wildest dreams did I think my acting career would lead to a successful modeling career. But, modeling helped me learn to work in front of a camera. Stage actors work in three dimensions; movie actors work in two dimensions. Modeling teaches you how you will look on film. Study the proof sheets photographers print of your photo sessions. You'll learn which angles and expressions work for you and which don't. I've known many great stage actors who have never been able to make the transition to film. They don't consider making themselves look good on camera their problem. They let the cameraman worry about that — or the makeup artist — or the lighting crew. A really good film actor knows how to make all these peoples' jobs easier. A really good film actor studies how his image turns out on film. Modeling makes you focus your attention on your work, one frame at a time. Modeling convinced my agents I could do film. Besides, modeling can be lucrative; don't turn your nose up at it if the opportunity arises. Hourly rates can be in the hundreds of dollars an hour, and you can expect to make bonuses for national print ads and billboards. Bonuses can range from hundreds of dollars to tens of thousands of dollars. When I was first approached by a modeling agency, I thought they were kidding. After a few years with them, I found myself doing a modeling job an average of once a week. It didn't get in the way of my theater work, and I found myself making as much money modeling for a few hours a week as I was making doing theater forty hours a week.

Commercials are the lifeblood of an acting career. Commercials are one of the largest and most important income categories for an actor. Actors who say they won't do commercials usually don't stay in the business very long. All actors do commercials — major stars included. Here are examples: Dustin Hoffman sold Volkswagens; Gene Hackman voiced United Airlines commercials; Donald Sutherland, Volvos; Michael Douglas, Infiniti. Bill Cosby did commercials for Jello and Coca-Cola. Alec Baldwin, Kris Kristoferson, and James Colburn voiced Chevrolet. Charlton Heston sold Budweiser, William Shatner sold Priceline.Com — the list goes on and on.

Television and radio commercials pay a major portion of all the monies earned by actors in Screen Actor's Guild and the American Federation of Television and Radio Artists. Commercials pay residuals. Residuals keep income flowing in for actors, so they can do things like eat and sleep indoors. In my career, I have done over 3,000 commercials. In other words, commercials have given me sixty to eighty days of work a year for the past twenty-eight years. Commercial jobs are lucrative one-day-long jobs that fill in many days of work between movies, television, and theater.

I could have been an industrial plumber, but I got involved in industrial theater and videos instead. This is another important area of work that provides a great deal of work for actors, and this area is rarely if ever mentioned by colleges. Most major companies have annual meetings and internal communication projects that use professional actors. Industrial shows are live theater performances at corporations' annual meetings. Many companies use musical comedy performers to energize these meetings. It's true that you may end up as a dancing hamburger in one of these meetings, but they generally pay a higher salary and offer better travel benefits than any other Actor's Equity contract. It is not unusual to find yourself in a world-class resort in Hawaii, Las Vegas, Nashville, or Florida with an industrial show company. Recently, I acted in a very unusual industrial show. I spent several days on a luxury liner in the Caribbean. It was more like a vacation than work. I still regularly perform in industrial shows. I do it for several reasons. I get to perform in front of big audiences. (The largest one was 17,000 live plus a national closed-circuit satellite feed.) Because the shows are live, there is a lot of pressure to be good — it tests your mettle. Because I do comedy, the audience lets me know if I am still funny and entertaining. And lastly, I keep my chops up without having to devote a lot of time to doing a play. In any case, industrial shows can be a pretty enjoyable way to augment your income. Being a dancing hamburger is a lot easier to take in world-class resort location.

Another area of industrial work is the corporate video. Most big companies need to make videos. Some of these videos are meant for internal use as training while others are public-image or sales videos. These videos are referred to as industrial films, and they are a great way to learn to act in films because they can provide you with lots of practical experience. It's better to be practical and acting than to be unemployed and wishing you were acting. Industrial films are nothing to turn your nose up at. John Cleese of *Monty Python* fame has concentrated a good portion of his career on creating comedy industrial videos. He created a company called Video Arts to market and distribute his industrial videos into more than thirty countries. His corporate videos have been regarded as the best in the business for the past two decades. For many years, Jim Henson's Muppets were one of the major producers of industrial films. Sure there are plenty of mundane industrial videos, but there are lots of mundane television shows and feature films, too. Industrial films can do a lot for your career if you use them to your advantage.

Once you begin to explore the job market, you'll find that there are many opportunities for an actor to find gainful employment for his or her talents. You just need to keep an open mind and be creative in your search. Here are some potential employers that most people don't consider on first thought: the opera, dance troupes, trade show companies, night clubs, comedy clubs, Las Vegas revues, broadcast companies (i.e., job opportunities as newspeople, weather people, talk shows, game shows, kid's show hosts, station announcers, disc jockeys, sportscasters), theme show parks, cruise ships, restaurants with performing waiters, and fashion shows. This is just a partial list. I assembled it by thinking of friends who went to acting schools and ended up doing the jobs listed as a way to make a living at some point in their careers. None of those actors thought they would end up doing those jobs, but they were all very grateful to do them because they were jobs that kept their careers alive at one point or another. The point to remember is that there are lots of jobs available for actors if you are willing to broaden your definition of what an actor does. Until you have a very established reputation, ideal acting jobs don't come along every day — or even every year. These kinds of jobs help you fill in the gaps. It allows you to practice your craft, and that is more productive than driving a cab. It's better to perform and be paid than to pay to perform in acting classes — you always learn the most from a live audience.

I Could Have Been an Accountant...

(Financing)

When I graduated high school, my advisor called me in to discuss my aptitude tests. He was very impressed with my scores. Even though I was in high school, he thought I could attain a higher level of employment than cabdriver. The results of my aptitude test were very clear. My advisor revealed that I had the talent to become an accountant. You see, I was very good at working with numbers. If I worked really hard, I might even be able to become a statistician. He also advised that the area I should avoid at all costs was anything involving the arts. The lowest scores on my aptitude test involved the arts. It was obvious: I had no talent. At the time I took these tests, I had not yet considered pursuing an acting career, so his comments didn't upset me very much. But, the thought of becoming an accountant didn't exactly thrill me. I enjoyed creative writing, but being creative with people's tax returns wasn't on my list of priorities.

It seems that my aptitude test showed that I was very organized. Supposedly, organization was good if you wanted to become an accountant, but bad if you wanted to become an artist. Personally, I haven't found my organizational ability getting in the way of my career. In fact, my desire to take the uncertainties out of my acting career are what led me to develop this practical guide to professional acting that I am presenting in this book. A systematic approach will dramatically improve an actor's chances of having a career. However, a lot of actors don't stick to the plan and eventually fail. (But that is because their high school advisors told them that their greatest aptitude was total disorganization, which made them likely candidates for careers in the arts.)

Throughout my career, many of my fellow actors have marveled at my ability to handle money. I know how to make it, I know how to keep it, and I know how to invest it to advance my career. My high school advisor was right. I definitely could have become a great accountant. I do have great aptitude in that area — and that single talent has made me unique among actors. I have stayed in business a very long time because my business has always been profitable. I operate in the black. Operating an acting business is like operating any other business. You need to have a regular source of income. Casey, my old stage manager friend, made me aware of this fact back at the Repertory Company. When the play was over, the income stopped. Good businesses plan ahead and never allow that to occur. To understand how to make money as an actor, you need to understand how the money is doled out. This is where a good accounting background comes in.

Actors make money in two ways. In the first way, they go to work and make money. In the second way, they go to work and make money and then make more money for a period of time after they have done their work. The second way is what successful actors spend most of their time doing. Remember this word: *RESIDUALS*. Residuals are monies you receive when your work is exhibited. To have a successful career, the major portion of your income needs to be residual based. In my case, 90 percent of my income is residual based. Only 10 percent comes from going to work. Let's examine this in detail.

As I mentioned, actors get paid for going to work. Some jobs pay residuals, but some do not. Jobs that usually do not pay residuals are theater, industrial shows, industrial videos, art films, comedy clubs, singing gigs, and so forth. Theater jobs are very attractive and spiritually rewarding, but they take up a lot of time, pay very little money, and are limited-term employment. You get a fair day's pay for a fair day's work; but when it's over, you're unemployed with no income. Theater pays a modest wage, and it is difficult to save money out of a theater paycheck. Theater is usually the reason most actors get interested in acting, but it is almost impossible to string together enough theater work to make a livable income. The other sources of employment I mentioned have a similar downside. They only pay while you stay employed. When you are young and first starting out, it is difficult to imagine a day when you will be too sick or too injured to perform. But those days do come along in every career. We've all blown our pipes at one time or another during the run of a play; and even Marcel Marceau has been left "speechless" because of a pulled muscle or two. You need to have a source of income during these times. This is where residuals become the key that can turn acting into a career.

Remember, if you show up for work, you get paid. More importantly, if your image shows up to work, you get paid. When your work plays on television, radio, or is rented on video, you get paid residuals. You can even get residual payments for still photos. I have appeared in films and television shows that have paid me residual payments for over twenty years! You get additional monies when movies are sold for video use. It's great when your feature film and television work brings in residual income, but commercials are the biggest single category of residual payment for actors. Generally speaking, if you do a commercial, you can expect payments minimally every thirteen weeks (three months) that your services are retained. It is not unusual for a commercial to provide income every thirteen weeks for a period of one to two years. Television commercials are the biggest single category, but radio commercials pay well, too.

Let me explain the impact that residuals can have on a career. Let's say that during the first six months of your career, you perform twelve days of work that can create residual income. You get paid for twelve days. Hardly enough to live on. During the next six months, let's say you work another twelve days. Again, hardly enough to live on, but the good news is you start to get residual payments from the first six months. In effect, you get paid for the twelve days you work plus residual payments that add twelve to twenty-four days of pay to your income. So, during your second six months, you're getting twenty-four to thirty-six days' pay. The goal is to continue adding residual days to your pay base until you are comfortable. After years of building your residual base, your residual income can grow to be bigger than your income from your day-to-day work. My ratio of residual income to work income is about nine to one. I work about 100 days a year; residuals bring in about 900 days of extra income. In effect, I get paid for 1,000 days of work a year — not bad work if you can get it. Because I am paid a livable wage all year round, I can pick and choose the jobs I want to do. If I feel like devoting a larger portion of my time to doing theater, I can because I can afford to. It is a nice position to find yourself in.

If all this sounds very confusing, don't worry. After all, this chapter was written by a guy who could have been an accountant. I wanted to live a normal life. (This might also be unusual for an actor.) I wanted to have a wife, a dog, a house, kids, and a comfortable lifestyle. I couldn't see myself sharing an apartment with another actor and worrying about the rent when I was forty. So, I used my organizational and accounting skills to learn everything there was to learn about residuals. That knowledge allowed me to develop a formula to figure out how to best utilize my time. How much of your job-hunting time do you devote to theater, to films and television, to industrial shows and videos, and to commercials? It all depends on how comfortable you want to be. Some people are happy with apartment life and roommates after forty; other people want a Malibu beach house and a Porsche at thirty. If you want the former, your ratio might be 90 percent work/10 percent residuals; if you want the later, you better plan on doing 1,000 percent work/1,000 percent residuals. If you want to have a long and profitable career as an actor, you have to make residuals a major portion of your financial picture.

CHAPTER TEN

I Could Have Been a Philosopher...
(Public Relations)

One night, at supper time, we were all gathered around the table discussing philosophy. I remember it well. My wife passed me the potatoes, and we got into a heated debate about existentialism. Of course, our ten-year-old had to put in his ten cents, which, of course, caused our teenage son to disagree. The debate raged on well into dessert. I disagreed with my wife, the kids disagreed with me and her, and, of course, with each other. After a short time, it was obvious that we were all going to need professional help. Thank goodness I went to college: I knew who to call for help. Obviously, a professional philosopher could settle this once and for all. I knew lots of people who went to school to get philosophy degrees. So, I left the table to get the telephone book. I looked in the classified ads under "philosophers" but, amazingly there wasn't a single one listed in the entire Chicago area. I thought: "What kind of town did we live in? This can't be!" I was probably looking under the wrong heading. I called information. "Where do I find a philosopher?" The operator paused before she answered: "I'll have to *think* about it! Try the Athens Restaurant and ask for Plato." Then she hung up.

Some people think an acting degree is a waste of time. Somehow, I have to guess that there are a lot more acting majors working at acting than philosophy majors working at thinking the kind of thoughts they thought they'd be thinking. In any case, I think it's a lot harder to find a philosopher than an actor. But, none of this diminishes the fact that it is harder to find acting work than it is to find actors. Believe it or not, one of the biggest problems in securing acting work is putting yourself in a position that producers can find you. Where do producers find actors? Actors don't place ads in the Yellow Pages of the telephone book. The don't advertise on billboards. . . or do they? (I'll get back to this idea in a little while.)

When producers cast projects, they look for actors. The bigger the project, the more important it is to get "a sure thing." What is "a sure thing"? At the highest levels, it is a bankable star. If you get a hot star for your movie, it will get a guaranteed audience even if your project stinks. However, when it gets down to the beginner level, a producer is just looking for an actor who he is confident can do the job (i.e., "a sure thing"). They begin the search for actors with casting directors and agents who assure them the actors who are auditioning are all capable of doing the job. The agent promotes the actor to the casting director, who in turn introduces the actor to the producer. That is the most common way actors get introduced to producers and casting directors.

However, there are many other ways that producers and directors find actors. Sometimes producers and directors see actors in plays, at comedy clubs, or in commercials, movies, or television shows. Sometimes, they ask other producers and directors for suggestions. Sometimes the writer of a project will recommend an actor — and sometimes, an actor already involved in the project will recommend you. But, one thing is very clear: You have to be known around the block to get in the game. If you hang around the game long enough, people eventually notice you. The real trick is finding where the game is and who to hang out with. In contemporary business lingo, this is called networking. You find out who is working and get to know them. They will be able to tell you what is going on around the block. The more people you know, the better idea you will have of what is going on.

The concept of networking sounds simple. But, it is a complicated art form that has many pitfalls and nuances. First of all, you must remember, actors tend to be very secretive about work. If you have a source of income, you don't want everyone else to know about it. Some producers have a very small group of favorite actors and tend to use them a lot. They don't always want to go through casting calls — using the same small group enables them to go with what they know works. Why fix it if it ain't broke? But producers are human. Confronted with the choice of a new toy, they sometimes discard the old one. (In fact, that was the plot of *Toy Story*, where the stars were toys voiced by stars.) So, actors tend to be protective of sources for employment; they don't want their favorite producers having choices instead of them. This is especially true if you happen to be the same "type" as the person you're trying to network with.

But networking is essential when you first start. After graduation, actors tend to stay in touch with one another. When I entered the business in Chicago, I had a lot of friends from Northwestern doing the same thing. I found that it was easiest to network with people competing for different parts than those I was auditioning for. They would tell me about work I was right for, and I would tell them about work they were right for. Sometimes these leads didn't work out, but it helped build a bigger base of potential clients for the future. As you build a business, you need to build a client list. A play every actor should read is *Glen Gary/Glen Ross* by David Mamet. It is a play about real estate agents and a list of potential clients. Every successful actor I know has a list. On this list are names of people who hire actors. After every job you do, write down the names of the producer, director, writer, creative director, or anyone else who might be able to help you find work someday. People in the business change jobs frequently. (When I was at The Second City, I used to do a lot of jobs for a writer at Leo Burnett Advertising whose name was John Hughes. If you've ever seen a John Hughes film, you know he eventually got a much better job.) Over the years, I have worked for several thousand clients, and I keep all their names on my list. I still have a network of actors I share information with. I belong to a voice-over performance ensemble, and we all compile information onto a master list that we all work from. It is kept on a computer and updated regularly so that we know who has gone where and who is doing what. It pays to stay in touch with people who have enjoyed working with you because they are likely to hire you again. In any case, having a list of potential employers is always a valuable asset.

OK, so let's get back to the billboard idea I mentioned a few pages back. To become known in a community should actors put their face on a billboard so producers know where to find them? One day, I was driving into Chicago on the main street that comes into the Michigan Avenue area — where the majority of producers, directors, and writers go every day — and I noticed that a billboard was vacant. I said to myself that would be a great place to put an ad to reach everybody who hires me! I have to admit, sometimes I scare even myself. I called everybody in my voice ensemble together and presented the idea. Everybody laughed and thought the idea was insane, so we decided to look into it. After all, everyone who hired us would think of us each day if we put ourselves on that billboard. So, we called the billboard company to find out what it would cost. When we found out it was going to cost $12,000 a month, we decided to rethink the idea. We noticed a bus bench under the billboard that said "Rent Me." The bus bench was $1,200 a year, so we took it. That bench became a Chicago landmark for the business for two years and became a constant reminder to everyone who passed it to hire us. The average man on the street didn't know what the bench was advertising, but it worked for us because enough of the people who hired us saw it each day. They thought it was funny and creative, and it made an impact. We got more jobs as a result, and a crazy idea worked.

Becoming an actor is greatly dependent upon your ability to become well-known. Actors are people who audiences want to see. That's why sports stars, super models, and bodybuilders frequently get to be actors. They've done things in other areas that give them top-of-mind presence. Their other talents are the "billboards" that make producers think of them first. Your acting skills might be far superior to theirs, but if the right people don't know about you it won't make a difference. If all you have to attract attention are your acting talents, pay special attention to the next chapter.

CHAPTER ELEVEN

I Could Have Been an Ad Man...
(Advertising)

When I was working at the repertory company during my senior year at Valparaiso University, something very interesting happened. It was opening night of the summer season when the head of advertising for the theater revealed that he had been too busy to prepare the advertising for the summer season. No advertisements had been placed to let people know what we were going to be doing plays that summer. As a result, in a 400-seat theater, we opened the season to about sixty people. The cast anticipated a large audience, and they were disappointed. But the executive producer was even more upset. He had more people backstage than in the audience. I talked to him and expressed my disbelief that the ad man could have been so inept. Even someone who knew nothing about advertising like myself knew more than this guy did. When the ad man walked in the door, it should have been a revolving door because he was out in less than five minutes. The executive producer fired him because he had found someone better. Imagine my surprise when I found out that someone was me! I had not expected or wanted the job, but since I opened my big mouth, I decided to make the best of the opportunity. I wanted to perform for an audience. All I needed to do was find one.

During your entire acting career, you will always be looking for an audience. Don't always expect someone to find one for you. Being in charge of advertising for a big theater really taught me how important and powerful a tool advertising and public relations can be for a career. Top-of-mind awareness is the goal of any advertising campaign. Reach the right audience with the right message and you make sales. Acting schools don't prepare you to write and produce advertising, but they should. If you're going to be a well-known actor, somebody has to get your name out in front of the public and the industry. If you're a big movie star, the job is simple; the studio does it for you. Publicists make sure *People* takes pictures of you and writes gossip about you and that *Entertainment Tonight* does stories about your new movie or play. The studio sends fans autographed pictures of you. You are a household word. However, when you are first starting out, you are your own publicist and advertising company.

Every actor has to establish an image in the marketplace. The bigger impact you make, the more opportunities you will get. In the beginning, you start with a head shot and résumé. For many actors, this is where advertising begins and ends. You send a picture and résumé out and wait for the phone to ring. If that is all the advertising you plan on doing, you will have a very, very long wait. Tens of thousands of head shots circulate yearly. If a producer wants a six-foot tall redhead who can roller blade and yodel, a casting director will have 100 pictures and résumés on that producer's desk the next day. Unless your picture fills a very select category, chances are that it will not be enough advertising to get you significant work. You need to do more.

If you are not a star, you need to learn to advertise and promote yourself. Most successful actors regularly budget advertising dollars into their expenses. Plan on spending 10 percent of your income on advertising. The more successful you become, the more you will spend. The larger your customer base, the more it will cost to reach them. I know actors in Chicago that spend in excess of $40,000 a year on advertising. Some actors hire writers who work in conjunction with graphic artists to act as small advertising agencies for them. Their job is to create an image and market it for the actor.

How do actors advertise? I already told you about my bench idea. It was unique, attracted a lot of attention, and was very affordable. But, it is not for everyone. Many actors use postcards. They have a postcard made of their head shot and use it to send thank-you notes or announcements. They send them to casting directors to thank them for asking them in for an audition or send them to clients to announce that they are appearing in a play or on a television show. Most actors can't afford fancy printed postcards, so they use xeroxed flyers instead. Some actors place ads in various publications. Most major cities have production bibles that contain a talent section for quick reference by producers. Ads like this contain the actor's picture and a memorable slogan that hopefully captures the essence of the actor. There are also national publications used by casting directors. Some actors choose to place ads in trade magazines and newspapers. I've seen actors take out ads in *Variety, Ad Age,* and *Screen.* Some actors like to leave little tchotchkes to remind producers of them. It is popular to leave pencils and pens with the actor's name on them. One announcer I know used to give producers stopwatches with his name and phone number on them. (Another announcer I know gave all the same producers a stopwatch holder with *his* name and phone number on it to put the other announcer's stopwatches in! Talk about a clever promotion!) Some actors go the social route. They take producers to lunch. Some actors throw theme parties; others rent skyboxes at sporting events. Some actors concentrate on doing things that attract news coverage. Sports come to mind, but publicity stunts work well, too. One of the students who had attended my seminars at Valparaiso University pulled a major prank on the Chicago theater critics. He was getting ready to open an original play and created a totally fictitious press release about the play's history and heritage as an ancient German clown art form. The critics bought it and gave the show four-star reviews. When word got out that he had suckered them, everyone had a good laugh; even the critics took it well since it was so much in keeping with the show. (He later opened a sequel to equally good reviews.) There are no set standards that actors use to advertise themselves. If you can come up with something unique and original, all the better.

A key point to remember is that you are advertising to sell your product. You need to really zero in on what you do or want to do. If you want to be a musical comedy performer, design your advertising to make the producer remember that aspect of your talent. Sometimes critics will give you a byline that will be memorable; sometimes you need to create your own byline. When you're advertising your talents, don't try to be all things to all people. If you're an ingénue, don't send out a picture of yourself looking like a mature businesswoman. Save that photo for your industrial clients. Producers go shopping for products. Make sure your advertising lets them know what your product is all about.

To illustrate what I mean, let me relate a story that helped one of my friends, Al Mitchell. Early in my career, I was doing a radio commercial for Hallmark Cards. I had the lead role. It was an emotional read, and I had done about sixty different takes for the client when the tag announcer arrived at the studio. A tag announcer says a slogan for the campaign at the end of the commercial. A single tag might be put on great numbers of commercials, and the tag announcer is paid for all of them. When the tag announcer arrived at the studio, the advertising agency people told me to take a break, because the tag announcer was very busy and only had a few minutes before his next session. He stepped into the recording booth and read one sentence about ten times in less than five minutes. The agency liked what he did and told him his tag would be edited into twelve commercials! In other words, he would make about twelve times more than I did in a fraction of the time. Sometimes, having the lead part isn't what it's cracked up to be. Anyway, I related my story to Al and said: "With your voice, you should market yourself as The Tag Man. Then when producers have tags, they'll think of you." Al created several promotions around this concept. He put tags on all his tape boxes and used the slogan "Play Tag with Al." Tag work poured in. He got to say exciting things like "Member FDIC" and "Check with your physician." Nothing to write home about, but it sure does pay the bills. The point is, he identified a need in the marketplace and exploited it with his advertising and promotional skills.

Are you running the risk of pigeonholing yourself? Yes. Can you end up getting type cast? Yes. But, that isn't all bad. When you are first starting out, you need to make people remember you for something. You might be remembered initially as "the funny guy with the real big nose," but that's better than being "the funny guy with the name and face I can't remember." As I mentioned earlier, you can always expand what you are remembered for. Because I never talked in the Cheer commercials I appeared in, many people wonder if I can talk. Many of the people I announce for wonder if I ever work on-camera. People that hire me for commercials are sometimes surprised that I act in plays and movies. People hire you to do things they are sure you can do. If you want to be a successful actor, establish a memorable image in the marketplace that lets people know what you do.

CHAPTER TWELVE

I Could Have Been an Executive...
(Management)

Some people go to work every day. They get dressed up in business suits and spend their days in meetings. They go to the same office every day and have regular schedules. They know what they will be doing six months or even a year ahead of time. They get regular paychecks, regular vacations; they have expense accounts and get company cars. If this sounds appealing to you, acting might not be the right profession for you. Even if you are somebody's father on a sitcom, life doesn't work out that way. For an actor, UNCERTAINTY is a way of life. Many people drop out of the performing arts because they find it difficult to cope with never knowing what is going to happen next. I must admit, it was a very scary issue to deal with when I first started my career. But once I figured out what the problem was, I was much more capable of dealing with it. The problem, simply put, is this: You are worried about what is going to happen next because you don't know what is going to happen. In other words, uncertainties are unpredictable. This isn't double-talk; it is reality. You can literally drive yourself crazy wondering about what will happen next.

So, what do you do? Learn to think like an executive. Executives spend a lot of time thinking about things that worry them. What will be the next hula hoop? What will the economy do next? Will the weather wreck the soybean crops? Are the pipe fitters going to go on strike? Who can I find that is willing to work for minimum wage — besides an out-of-work actor? Remember, each actor is responsible for his or her career. If you want to be a great actor, think like a big executive. If you just want to get by, think like a mom-and-pop grocery store. The better you get at asking yourself hard questions about UNCERTAINTY, the better you will become at creating a career for yourself. The good news is you don't have to wear a suit for your executive position because you are your own boss.

Thinking about uncertainties is not as hard as you might imagine. Set aside an hour to make some lists:

1) Things I'd like to do
2) Things I'd do if I can't do the things I'd really like to do
3) Things that stand in the way of doing the above

This is what executives do all day long. First, they create their dream product (things I'd like to do); then they compromise their original idea (things I'd do if I can't do the things I'd really like to do); and finally, they spend the rest of their careers trying to keep manufacturing their product without going bankrupt (things that stand in the way of doing things I do since I can't do the things I'd really like to do). Plan your dream career — make your dream spectacular because you will have to compromise your ideal. Then identify the roadblocks that will stand in your way. It is sort of like playing chess. The farther ahead you can foresee problems the better you will be able to deal with them. What are some foreseeable problems?

"Save ahead for a rainy day." Most actors' businesses fail because of poor financial planning. They run out of money. Their business bankrupts. If your business runs out of money, you are out of business. Actors then become cabdrivers or waiters to pay the bills. Because they are pursuing a new career, they no longer have time to act. This situation deserves very serious attention. Never allow yourself to run out of money! Would you go to a doctor who couldn't afford to keep his practice open? Would you let a lawyer defend you who had to drive a cab to keep his law practice going? Would you hire a carpenter who couldn't afford a hammer? Is it any wonder that producers are reluctant to hire actors who are difficult to get a hold of because their phones are disconnected or they are unreachable because they are off doing their full-time jobs?

If you are going to open a business, have a bankroll behind it. Work a hundred hours a week if necessary so that you have money to invest in your career. You'll need money for pictures, résumés, clothes, grooming necessities, an answering service, a pager, classes, and union dues not to mention living expenses while you spend all your daytime hours looking for work. You need money to open your business. If you don't have money, it is like opening a grocery store without having money to buy groceries to stock the shelves with. You can't wait to see what the customers want; if you're open for business, you need to be ready to deliver. Nothing is worse than having a young actor win an audition and then not be able to do the job because he or she cannot afford to join the union. Plan on having at least three thousand dollars set aside to join Screen Actors Guild (SAG), The American Federation of Television Radio Artists (AFTRA), and/or Actor's Equity Association

(AEA). Gaining admission to the acting profession is an expensive proposition for a reason: to keep out people who want to do it as a lark. If you want to do this as a profession, be prepared to make a massive investment of money, time, and effort. If you're going to open a business, do it right. Have sufficient funds to keep your business open.

OK, the last paragraph was a little rough on you. It's true, I'm a good businessman. I am comfortable in financial meetings at major corporations. I know what I am talking about, and I don't pull any punches. Don't hate me for it. The vast majority of actors don't think about financial planning. Acting schools don't offer courses on this subject. I'm sorry I've got to be Mr. Bad News. How many famous actors have gone bankrupt? Lots and lots! The reason is simple: financial planning. Look ahead. Put pencil to paper and figure how much money you need to keep your business open. My personal rule of thumb is to have a minimum of the money needed for six months set aside for rainy days. As an actor, you will experience a lot of rain. To calculate how much money you will need, estimate how much money it would take to pay all your bills for the upcoming six months. Budget liberally because we always spend more money each succeeding six-month period. The more money you make, the more money you will spend. Every business is this way. Here is a sample list:

SIX MONTHS' EXPENSES FOR THE BEGINNING ACTOR
Rent
Electric and Gas
Food
Entertainment/Restaurants
Grooming (Hair/nails/makeup)
Telephone Bill
Answering Service/Cell Phone/Pager
Union Dues for SAG, AFTRA, and AEA

Agent's Fees (10 percent of the money you make)
Acting Classes
Dance Classes
Exercise Classes
Automobile Expenses:
    Car payments, Gas, Insurance, Repairs, Parking
Out-of-Town Expenses: (If you look for work in other cities)
    Airfare, Hotels, Food
Clothing Budget
Advertising and Promotion Budget:
    Pictures, Résumés, Mailings
Student Loans
Medical Bills
Unpleasant Surprises

Six months of expense money may seem like a lot, but realistically, it is a minimum amount. Everyone's expenses will be different, so I can't really give you any specific dollar amount to plan on. The best way to arrive at a figure is to look at what you spent in the previous six months. Get out your checkbook and charge account statements and write the numbers down — and don't forget about all the cash you went through. Above all, don't guess at the numbers! Numbers don't lie. When we don't look numbers up, we all tend to make them what we want them to be rather than what they really are. Don't be optimistic about how little you can get by on. The unpleasant surprises category at the end of the list has wrecked many a budget. A refrigerator or washing machine needs to be replaced, the engine falls out of your car, your dog eats a steak bone whole and needs an operation, your son gets a French fry stuck up his nose and a doctor has to get it out — these are all unexpected surprises that threw a monkey wrench into my financial projections at the least opportune times of my career. But, the very fact that I budgeted for unpleasant surprises made it a lot easier to survive the ordeal. (The dog's operation was over $1,000!) Plan on going through this little ritual every six months for your entire career. I still do it with regularity. Never take the finances of your business for granted. The more money you make, the more money you will spend; the more money you spend, the more money you will need to make: It is part of a vicious cycle driven by human nature. (Used-car lots in Hollywood are filled with Ferraris actors thought they could afford until they discovered an oil change can cost $1,000.) Your financial picture is ever-changing; spend time studying it. The more financially secure you are, the better chance you will have of succeeding at your acting career.

Once your store is open, you will need to spend all your days and nights looking for work. You will not have time to do anything else. In the beginning, the searching for work will consume all your energies and finances — and, most importantly, you need to be free to accept the work if you find it. Agents don't like working with actors who have to juggle work schedules with acting schedules. Your work must be your acting. Be open for business. Take a cab to your job; don't let the cab be your job. There is no shortage of people looking for acting work. If you ever spend any time in New York or Los Angeles, you will find that the streets are filled with people claiming to be actors. Every cabdriver and waitress will tell you that they are actors waiting for their big break. It is an easy thing to say you are an actor; it is a far more difficult thing to actually be an actor. To be an actor, you have to spend your time acting. Job hunting is the only way to find acting work. It is your first, last, and only activity anytime that you are not working as an actor. Until you are an established star, jobs will not search for you; you must search for jobs. Quite frankly, even stars work hard at getting the roles that are really choice. Early in your career, it is important to understand that the majority of the time and effort you will expend on your acting career will be spent looking for work — not acting. Looking for acting work is hard; doing acting work is easy. Great numbers of people want to be actors because the work is very enjoyable and rewarding. Very few people get to be actors because the search for acting work is very difficult and frustrating. The first step in having a successful acting business is understanding that your full-time job is looking for work; this first step is also the most difficult challenge. It is not easy waking up each morning knowing that you are unemployed and must find work. Most people find this very traumatic. Most people who work regular jobs only have to do it a few times in their entire lifetime. Actors, on the other hand, have to do it each and every day of their lives.

Be Prepared. Every good business is ready for the busy season. Stores get ready for Christmas in August. If you're out looking for work in musical theater, you better be ready to sing and dance. When a producer is looking for a tapper, they'll find one the next day; they won't be willing to wait two weeks for one to get in shape. If a producer is looking for a blonde with long hair and has selected you from your head shot that shows you with long blonde hair, don't show up with a buzz cut and say you can grow the hair back in six months. Keep your chops up; take voice, dance, and acting classes. Keep your appearances up; look like your head shot. You are a product. If you found orange soda in a can of Coca-Cola, you would not be happy. Be prepared to do what you've told people you can do. On a project I was producing, an agent told me one of her talents could do an incredible Tarzan yell. When I auditioned the actor, he assured me he could do anything. He couldn't do it. He wasn't even close. He looked like a fool, and I learned never to trust his agent at her word. Quality control is very important to every business. It is a pleasure to do business with reputable companies. Be able to deliver what you promise.

There is a second very important aspect to being prepared. Things happen very quickly in the acting business. One day you don't have a television series, the next day you do. One day you are in your one-bedroom apartment in Chicago, the next day you're living in a hotel room in Los Angeles — in fact, the next six months you're living in that hotel room in Los Angeles. When you audition for something, you need to be prepared to adjust your life accordingly. Your life revolves around your work — not your work around your life. Film work happens like a train wreck; it happens fast, it's huge, and when it's over, it's over — there is a very small window of opportunity for you to be involved with it. When someone asks you to do a job, you have to be prepared to say "yes" and drop everything on a moment's notice. Producers don't care about your personal life; they care about their project. They want actors who have no strings attached. They don't have time to wait while you get your personal problems settled. You always have to be prepared to have someone or a service in place to take care of things like your apartment, your dog, watering your plants, making sure your kids get to school on time, and so forth. Have a plan in place at all times to cover your personal life. This may sound cruel, but it's reality. Many actors personal lives are in shambles because they seem irresponsible. They are expected to pick up and go when they are called. Actually, actors who are working professionals are more responsible to their work than any other profession. There is an old theater expression that sums it all up: "An actor can die, but he can't miss his entrance." Take being-prepared-to-work-at-a- moment's-notice very seriously.

Keep Your Options Open. Businesses have to change with the market. There will be acting jobs you will want to do and acting jobs you won't want to do. There will be acting jobs you will want to do but won't be able to afford to do. There will be acting jobs that you will hate but will pay more money than you can afford to turn down. There will be acting jobs that you desperately want to do but can't afford to do but will do anyway because they are important to your career. You get the picture. These are management decisions that need to be made in every career. To make them, put pencil to paper. If you've saved for a rainy day, you'll be able to afford taking a low-paying artistic choice that is important to you. If you're living hand to mouth, you might need to take a good-paying acting job you're not interested in over an artistically satisfying one because you need to fuel your business with money. Choose the option that is best for your business.

Throughout your career, the pattern of your work will change. Some areas of business will dry up for you, and others that were previously not open to you will become a major source of your income. You will grow older; your look will change; your voice will change; your type will be in style and then out of style; you may develop an untapped talent in classes; a new form of media might develop that is perfect for you. (Silent film actors lost work to theater actors when talkies evolved; radio performers found a new source of income in television; maybe some of us will find new work in holograms in the near future.) It is important to always be open to new business opportunities. These opportunities may not be your first priority, but they might develop into a major source of your income and become your "thing." Be ready to change with the times; be ready to modify your product.

Managing an acting career is more difficult than managing a business that sells packaged goods because you are your product. It is difficult to be a detached observer of yourself. How many times have you heard people say: "I'm my own worst critic!" If you want to be a successful actor, you need to learn to be your own best critic. You know what you want to become. Be honest with yourself and improve your short-comings. Look at your career as a company would look at its business.

Where does your company need the most help? Is your product good enough? Is your company financially strong? Do you have good sales and marketing? Is your business plan well organized? These questions are not any fun to answer, but if you do ask and answer them regularly, you will be better prepared to deal with the UNCERTAINTIES of an acting career.

CHAPTER THIRTEEN

I Could Have Been a Psychiatrist...
(Managed Health Care)

When I was on tour with The Second City, we played an extended engagement in Cleveland. We all lived together in a large Victorian house on the banks of Lake Erie. It was a truly beautiful place even though the Cayahoga River caught on fire that summer from pollutants. Anyway, living and performing with the same group of actors for six weeks was a very interesting experience. One day I had spent my morning visiting ad agencies looking for some commercial work to supplement my income; when I returned to the house, a few of the cast members called me into the library to have a little talk. They had a problem with me. They couldn't understand why I was happy all the time. I was cheerful; I was happily married; I loved my wife and my dog; I had a condominium; I worked all the time; I got to work on fun stuff; I didn't see a shrink; I didn't have a drug or alcohol problem; I was rarely depressed. What was the matter with me? Didn't I want to have a career badly enough to be willing to suffer like them? Shouldn't I have as much trouble in my life as they were having in theirs? This was a surreal moment in my life. These people were all dead serious. I sat in stunned silence as this bizarre scene played out. Then one by one they began to apologize for what they had just said. Tears were held back. They said what they did was terrible, and they were all sorry. They said they did it because they were all so screwed up. As I sat there and listened, I understood. I felt everything that they felt; I just never let it get to me. I was like a psychiatrist: I observed but did not let myself become emotionally involved. I guess this is why I would have made a good accountant, too. When you work with numbers, you don't get emotional. You work through the calculations and get a logical result. The numbers work out like the numbers work out, and then you deal with it.

Acting is a funny business. It is very hard to balance logic and emotion. We make our livings portraying emotions, and we are rewarded for displaying them. Perhaps actors are more emotional than other people. But if you are going to have an acting career, it is best not to become emotional about the business of emotions. I have had a very successful career. I have won hundreds of auditions. However, I have lost thousands of them. Sometime when you have nothing to do, practice walking into room and saying: "Hi, honey, I'm home. I lost my audition today." Do it a thousand times allowing yourself to feel the geniune remorse and disappointment an actor actually feels after losing an audition and see how you feel. Stress the word *lost* each time you say it. Get used to it. No matter how good you are, you will lose many auditions. There is no second place in acting. There will be times when you will audition against hundreds of other actors. The odds are not good; but many of us survive and make very good livings and lead wonderful, happy lives.

Dealing with failure is difficult for any business. Because

you are your product, it is especially difficult. Actors take rejection personally. (How else can you take it?) If you want to succeed, you need to learn to deal with rejection. After twenty years of professional acting, I took an audition class to focus my skill of auditioning. (You're never too successful or smart to learn.) The instructor was a casting director, and he said something that really stuck with me. He said that if a casting director puts an actor on a casting call, that actor is good enough to do the job. The casting director and director are both hoping each actor will be perfect for the part so they can progress with the job. Whether or not you win the part depends on things beyond your control. Some people like soup with pepper; others don't. Some people like actors with freckles; other don't. The very fact that you were asked to audition means that someone thinks you're good enough to do the job. If you perform up to snuff in auditions, people will ask you back again and again; the odds will begin to turn in your favor. The statistician in me has always found this to be a ray of hope that keeps me going. I keep a record of auditions and my win/lose ratio. If you keep getting auditions, it means your agent, casting directors, producers, directors, and writers believe in you, and eventually you'll get work. Learn to look for the silver lining in every cloud. Sometimes that is all you will get to keep you going. I have always tried to find the positive in every experience even if it means learning from my mistakes. The more you audition and experience winning and losing first hand, the better you will become at it. Hopefully, you will be a much better auditioner after your one-hundredth audition than you were after your first. Losing is much harder than winning; it hurts and it pays less. But, win or lose, you need to be able to develop a healthy attitude about success and failure.

I am not a psychiatrist. I am not an overly emotional person. Maybe that's why I don't suffer quite as acutely as most

actors seem to after losing an audition. It's not that I don't care. It's not that I have ice water in my veins. It's not that I have a high threshold for pain. I think I handle the stress of competition and failure in an analytical way. I spend a lot of time studying numbers like an accountant. I keep track of my successes and failures. I know which areas I succeed in, and I focus more of my effort and attention on those areas. When I have too many failures in a certain area, I am smart enough to vary my approach until I see the writing on the wall. For example, when I was just doing plays, I knew I could always find work in theater. After a time, I had enough of a reputation that I did not have to spend a great amount of time and effort finding theater work; it found me. So, I turned my attention to finding a new area of work. I explored on-camera commercials and voice-overs because I discovered that there were many auditions for each in Chicago. The biggest agent in Chicago told me to forget voice-over work, but a smaller agent gave me shot at it. Because my voice was higher than most people in the voice-over business, I quickly found a regular spot in the Chicago voice-over business as an alternative to the smoother baritone voice-over actors that dominated the business at that time. The point is don't beat your head against a brick wall. Explore many different ways to make your living as an actor. Work hard to find your niche. A lot of actors think themselves into a corner. Because they're not doing leads in feature films, they get depressed. Find something you can win at. It will give you an income, and you'll feel better about yourself.

Another thing that has helped me enormously as an actor was having someone to talk to. Some actors talk to their shrinks. Some actors talk to their spouses. Some actors talk to their agents. Some actors spend fortunes calling home. Many times actors talk among themselves (it's funny how sometimes you can see yourself by talking to someone who has the same

problem). Some actors talk to their pets. Remember, you don't have to be a ventriloquist to talk to yourself. Don't keep things bottled up inside yourself. Find someone who is interested in listening to you grouse. I've never been to an audition where a group of actors were not congregated together and complaining about something. I think my favorite such session happened in New York. A group of New York actors were complaining about the way Fettuccine Alfredo was prepared in the Midwest. Each actor had a more horrific story than the next. Iowa, Nebraska, and Illinois were ranked as the worst places on Earth for Fettuccine Alfredo. Everyone shared a common hatred; everyone left the audition feeling great. No one cared who won or lost the audition; everyone bonded and felt stronger — except me, who still lived in Chicago and had to return home with an unnatural fear of Fettucine Alfredo.

Another thing that has helped me manage rejection depression is always having an available outlet for frustration. I have always been an athlete. There is nothing like extreme physical activity to take your mind off your problems. Whatever works for you is good. Personally, I like ice hockey, dance classes, and running. All three push me to the point of physical exhaustion. Tony Danza, Robert Conrad, and Donny Osmond box. Jane Fonda does aerobics. I have never been to a city where actors don't have highly competitive softball teams. Have an outlet you enjoy that allows you to blow off steam and physically accomplish something that makes you feel proud. I set mileage and speed goals for myself with my running. If I had a bad week, I would work the bad feelings out of my system by running farther and faster. Once I hit a plateau, I would change activities and find something new to conquer. Feeling like I was making progress at something kept me in positive spirits. As crazy as it might sound, even painting your house might give you a feeling of accomplishment so you can keep going. I've actually done it, and it has worked for me.

Unfortunately, a lot of actors turn their feelings of frustration to negative ends. Their feelings of frustration and failure make them turn to alcohol, drugs, sex, and violence in very negative ways. When that happens, it is a sad end to many careers. One of my friends played the lead on a successful series for five years. When the series was over, he didn't know what to do with himself. Drinking matched his macho image, so he poured all his efforts into drinking and having sex with adoring female fans. After a year, he had put on forty pounds and lost his wife. When his agent started to find him opportunities, people couldn't believe he was the same guy. No one could talk him out of his destructive lifestyle. He wouldn't talk about it with anyone. Word of his negative behavior spread out to the industry, and it destroyed his career. Think of all the actors you have read about in *People* magazine or the *National Enquirer* who have suffered a similar fate. Supermarket tabloids thrive on the aberrant behavior of celebrities. How can actors who have everything going for them throw it all away because of such destructive, foolish behavior? It is very sad, but it happens every day. Compared to other occupations, a disproportionate number of actors seem to turn to destructive lifestyles. Why do they do it? Acting can give you unbelievably gratifying highs and emotionally devastating lows. Everyone finds a different way of dealing with them. Some people find positive ways; others find negative ways. Some find God, some have out of body experiences, some believe in crystals, some become exercise fanatics, while others go overboard with alcohol, sex, and drugs. They are all ways of dealing with pressure and depression. I recommend choosing one of the ways that won't kill you.

Dealing with rejection is difficult, but it is something every actor must learn to do. If acting is all you have, it makes life even more difficult. Friends and family are important to your career. Other interests like sports and hobbies are positive out-

lets for your frustrations and pent-up energies. Don't lose the forest for the trees. While acting may be your main thing, don't let it be your only thing. Remember, you work to live; you don't live to work. Have a nice life. If you are fortunate enough to actually earn a living as a professional actor, revel in that. It has always been more than enough to keep me happy. Take great pride in the successes you achieve. Remember, not everyone gets to be a professional actor.

CHAPTER FOURTEEN

I Could Have Been a Masochist...
(Changing Careers)

D id you ever hear the one about the sadist and the masochist? My high school English teacher told it to me during a vocabulary-building lesson. A masochist walks up to a sadist and says: "Hit me! Beat me! Abuse me! I deserve it! Please do it!" The sadist considers it for a moment, smiles an evil smile and says: "No!" She was a pretty smart teacher. She never took teaching so seriously that it couldn't be fun. With one joke, I learned two new words. I also learned about two new types of people I had never heard of before. It seemed hard to believe that masochists could possibly exist. What kind of person would enjoy having people treat them abusively? How could anyone find that fun? It's true that actors frequently feel abused because they feel rejected every time they lose an audition. It's a natural reaction — but you don't have to like it or enjoy it.

Why does a person become an actor? For a lot of actors, it

starts when they are very young; they learn that it is very enjoyable being the center of attention. A little kid does something cute and everyone "oohs" and "ahhhhs." They do it over and over until their audience doesn't respond. Then they try something new to try and get a bigger and better reaction. They are drawn to the spotlight and enjoy the focus it gives them. They enjoy having people watch them and listen to them. They enjoy the positive feedback it gives them. Everyone likes attention and getting stroked. I think actors like it a little more than the average person. In any case, it's a part of being an actor. When people are always looking at you and listening to you, it gives you a feeling of pride, accomplishment, and importance. It makes you feel loved and wanted. Having an audience laugh at your jokes and applaud your performances provides a wonderful feeling that is hard to duplicate any other way. Seeing your picture on the front of a magazine or on a motion picture screen or television set is an unbelievable sensation. Seeing your name up in lights is an incredible thrill. The first time I experienced each one of these things is something I will never forget. Once an actor experiences these sensations, it is very hard to give them up. In fact, it is the ultimate rush for many actors.

However, you do not always get the satisfaction of experiencing these things. Even if you are a major star, life is not one continuous high after another. There is the moment of exhilaration and then there are all the moments of hard work and tedium in between those incredibly wonderful moments. As I've already mentioned, most of your time will be spent looking for work rather than experiencing the smell of the grease paint and the roar of the crowd. No one will applaud your sales efforts as you search for work. No one will make you feel wanted or loved as you make cold calls. You will not feel a rush of pleasure as you address and stamp your publicity pieces, head shots, and résumés. All in all, it takes a lot of ungratifying, humdrum, tedious work to find your way to the spotlight, so you better have a little bit of the masochist in you.

It is a good idea to do a little soul-searching before you decide to make acting your profession. Why do you want to become an actor? A lot of people do it because they like the attention — "Look at me! I'm wonderful!" Parents and relatives laugh and applaud and tell you that you are wonderful. At school, you become the class clown or you start dressing in all black, wearing a cape and looking very serious all the time; everyone at school notices you because you are different. You act weird and do things the other kids don't do. You love the attention. Actors love attention. So, you are going to be an actor because actors get all the attention.

We've all experienced high school and community theater groups. They are filled with the kind of actors I've just described. The universe was created to revolve around them. When you're a kid, it's cute. If you plan on being a professional, it's not. Don't become an actor because you crave attention. Producers, directors, writers, agents, managers, and other professional actors are very busy people who have a lot to do. They don't have time to pay attention to needy people who want to be stroked. If you are becoming an actor because you crave attention, you will be very disappointed. I mention this because I have seen this happen many, many times. People become actors to get more attention and then they get crushed when they don't get it. Producers aren't sadists by trade, but they only have one job for all the actors that audition. More people lose than win, so most of them are going to be very disappointed and feel very unwanted.

Unfortunately, I have met many actors with very unhealthy attitudes. In a very masochistic way they actually learn to thrive on failure. They begin to enjoy it. I call it the Marilyn Monroe complex. In a lot of Marilyn Monroe's films, she played a beautiful woman who just couldn't find anyone who would love her. She was so sweet and beautiful, how could anyone not possibly love her? She was stuck in a deadend job, overworked, neglected, and lonely. How could life be so unfair? Everyone felt sorry for her. I have seen tremendously talented actors who weren't getting the breaks start to rationalize their failures. When they lost auditions they obviously should have won, friends would feel sorry for them and faun over them. "How could someone as talented as you lose? Life is so unfair!" It is sad when actors begin to crave the attention they get when they lose an auditon. Their art is not as important as having people feel sorry for them. They are more interested in being the center of attention than acting.

Because acting is such an emotionally demanding profession, I don't recommend doing it if your only motivation is the self-gratification of getting attention. That is certainly a starting point for many actors. But eventually you need to have more motivating you to get you past the hard work of finding work. Many actors drop out during the first year of looking for work because rejection is just the opposite of what they are searching for. Pushing forward seems very masochistic. Why go out to get abused and overlooked? I went to school with many actors who I thought were far better actors than I. Many of them quit early in their careers because they were not getting what they wanted. They didn't get the praise and attention they got in school. They went from being a big fish in a small pond to being a little fish in an ocean. They didn't get the big money they thought they'd earn. They didn't like the endless process of looking for work. The art of acting wasn't enough. Eventually, they turned to other occupations.

If you want to be a professional actor, you have to love the craft of acting more than anything else. You have to be 100 percent committed to succeeding no matter what. You have to be willing to deal with the inevitable frustration of rejection and losing auditions. You have to understand that you will always live under pressure to win. If you do not win, you will not earn money. If you do not win, your agent may stop sending you on auditions. You have to accept that there are more people who want to be actors than there are jobs available. You have to realize that no one is going to look out for you or manage your business. You have to live with the fact that you are replaceable. You have to be aware that the world does not revolve around you. No one is obligated to pay attention to you. Producers hire actors to do acting jobs. Make sure that you want to become an actor because you are interested in the art of acting. That has to be enough to satisfy you and keep you going, because that is all you are going to get most of the time. The end of the rainbow for many people is becoming a well-known star. It is true that those people get a lot of attention, adulation, fame, and fortune. But not every actor gets that far. For the vast majority of professional actors, their love of the profession is what keeps them going. Before you begin this arduous, emotionally draining journey, ask yourself if that is enough for you. If it is, be a masochist and keep on reading!

CHAPTER FIFTEEN

I Could Have Been a Handicapper...

(Evaluating the Competition and the Marketplace)

I grew up in Cicero, Illinois, in the shadow of two racetracks, Hawthorne and Sportsman's Park. When I was a kid, I used to beg my Dad to drive past the track so that I could see a racehorse. They built the tracks so that it was impossible to see the horses from the street. But, one day I got lucky. A trainer had a horse on a strip of grass near the street away from the track. It is a sight I've never forgotten. The horse was magnificent! It was more beautiful than I ever imagined it was going to be. Until then, the only horses I had ever seen were cowboys' horses on black-and-white television sets or farm horses. I thought those horses were really something, but this horse was incredible compared to those! His coat glistened in the sun, and he looked so sleek compared to all the other horses I had seen. Best of all, he looked really, really fast.

In retrospect, I guess I shouldn't have been surprised because I was looking at a genuine thoroughbred racehorse!

Several actors who were completing university studies have apprenticed under me to study the business of acting. Mandatory reading for each of these students has been *Ainsle's Complete Guide to Thoroughbred Racing*. To be a successful actor, you don't need to know a lot about thoroughbred racing, but it helps to know the basics. First of all, only thoroughbred racehorses can race in thoroughbred races. Each of these horses was born to race. It is in their blood and they know it. While all thoroughbred racehorses are superior racers, they are not equal. It is possible to buy one thoroughbred racehorse for $200, and it is impossible to buy another thoroughbred racehorse for $2,000,000. The difference in speed between these two animals might be negligible, yet one is a champion and the other is not. The most expensive horses are called stakes horses. Their owners believe in them so much, they are willing to stake large sums of money that they will win. They race the most lucrative races. The next level of horse is the handicap horse and then the allowance horse. After that, there are various levels of claiming horses. (If you are a registered thoroughbred owner, you can claim the horse at the end of the race for the amount of money the horse has raced for. Claiming horses can be bought for tens of thousands or mere hundreds of dollars.)

All these different types of horses are thoroughbred race horses, they are similar in speed but vary greatly in worth. What separates them? Class. This is what Ainsle says class is:

> Thoroughbred class, or quality, is easy to recognize and hard to define. . . . the horses of the highest class — the champions — have been the ones whose physical soundness, speed, stamina and competitive willingness enabled them to beat everything in sight. They won under serious weight disadvantages. They

won on off-tracks. They won by narrow margins after over-coming serious lack of running room in the stretch. And, sometimes they won by exhausting their opponents in the first three quarters of a mile and romping home all alone, a city block in front.

Many of the horses they whipped were every bit as sound. Some were speedier. Some had no less stamina and as much courage. But champions combined those traits in maximum quantity. . . . Not many trainers can make a champion out of a potential champion.

Ainsle's Complete Guide to Thoroughbred Racing
by Tom Ainsle, published by Simon & Schuster,
pp. 192–193

I am sure Tom Ainsle wasn't thinking about actors when he wrote that paragraph, but I was when I read it. Class is a presence every star brings to every job. Class is present in every star, and it gives each of them an unmistakable glow. They have a confidence that commands attention. Other actors on the set might be better trained, better looking, or in better shape, but the seas part when the star takes the stage. Old champions beat young champions on class. Class can not be seen, but it sure can be felt. Every actor wants to be a star; every actor thinks that they should be a star. But very few ever attain the highest levels of stardom.

All professional actors are thoroughbreds; you know if you've got what it takes or not. Just like horses, all actors are cut from the same mold; it just takes some experience to see where you fit into the big picture. Stakes horses are like movie stars — they are very special and there are very few of them; that's why they get the big bucks. TV stars are like handicap horses — they are really good, but they are not movie stars.

Theater stars are like allowance horses. The majority of actors fall into the claiming horse category — a thoroughbred in every sense of the word, but not ready for any of the above categories. Some people never get to be stars. There's nothing wrong with that. As long as you're earning a living and doing what you like, so what? I am a commercial star. I have starred in theater, but not with regularity. When I was at The Second City, everyone assumed I would be a TV star with a sitcom. It hasn't happened. Almost all the sitcoms are done in L.A., and I haven't wanted to relocate my family to L.A. So, I do what I can do in Chicago and do the best I can with the opportunities I get. I live a very comfortable, happy life, and I have more than my share of success.

I know people who are stars of the industrial video business. They are unbeatable at what they do. They are proud of what they do. Bozo, the clown, is a friend of mine. He is a star of children's television that millions of people have grown up watching and loving. I have had the opportunity to work with him on other projects and have discovered that he is a very good actor. I think he deserves other bigger opportunities. But because he is a clown, hardly anyone knows what he looks like; so he gets limited opportunities to do other things. Some people become stars of voice-over. No one outside the business knows who they are even though they make a star's income, but they do not get the acclaim a star gets. The important thing to remember is that you may not become the kind of actor you dreamed of becoming. Be thankful for every success you have because many actors never have any successes. If you keep working, there is always the chance you may move up in class; someday you may achieve your dream. Getting to where you want to be in your career might take months, years, decades, or even a lifetime. If you're good enough to be a working actor, the hope of stardom will always move you forward.

Let's take a closer look at what it means to be a thoroughbred. Only thoroughbreds get to race in thoroughbred races. That is the minimum requirement. The same is true for professional actors. The very least that is expected of you is that you are the best there is. It is very difficult for many beginning professionals to understand this. While you are still in school, it is possible to out act your competition. You can be noticeably better than other actors trying out for the same role. But don't kid yourself — you are a thoroughbred racing against a field of plow horses. Once you get to the professional level, that is not very often the case. Everyone auditioning will be as good as you are. Everyone auditioning is a thoroughbred. Some thoroughbreds have more class than others, though. Some actors walk into an audition with more confidence and panache than everyone else. They impress the producer and director with those qualities. An actor's confidence level rises and falls depending on the competition. If you walk into an audition and everyone is a famous star and you are not, your confidence level might waver. But don't let situations like this throw you. Remember that someone thinks you should be there. It is your time to prove to everyone that it is your time to move up in class.

It is very interesting to watch auditions. Because I act, write, direct, and produce, I've observed auditions from many different viewpoints. On any given audition, I find that 85 percent of the actors reading for the role are perfectly capable of doing the job. Many of them attack the role in the same way. Typically, one or two of the actors will make unusual choices in an attempt to be different from everyone else; sometimes this strategy works and sometimes it doesn't. But overall, there are very slight differences in quality between the actors' auditions. As I mentioned earlier, the difference between a million-dollar stakes horse and an inexpensive claiming horse is sometimes less than a second or two. The difference between a movie star and an industrial video star is not that great either. I know that sounds hard to believe, but it is true. Some of the actors I worked with at The Second City went from doing a stage show for a few hundred dollars a week to movie careers where they made millions of dollars a film in just a few short years. It was all a matter of getting into the right position. Claiming horses need to work their way up the ladder to get shots at stakes races. Don't expect to be reading for leads in motion pictures a week after graduation. You need to prove yourself at each level of work. One of my favorite racehorses was Frosty Scott. The first time he raced at Arlington Park, he won a $5,000 claiming race. Each race he ran, he moved up in class. By mid-summer he was racing stakes races. All in all he won fifteen races and finished second once. He won the championship that summer at the fastest racetrack in the United States. In a match race, he beat a million dollar colt named Satan's Poppy. Frosty Scott looked like a police horse, but he had the heart of a champion. In the match race, he refused to give up the lead. He was the class, and when the chips were down, he proved it. I tell you the story of Frosty Scott to assure you that miracles happen, so never give up hope. You won't know what is in you until you are tested against the best. It takes time and opportunity to find out what you're made of. You will win auditions and you will lose auditions. Eventually, you will find a level of work where you win consistently.

There is an old expression you should always keep in mind: Different horses for different courses. Just because you are very successful at one thing does not mean you will automatically be successful at something else. Your star might rise in one area and never get off the ground in another. Many great Broadway actors never make it to the silver screen. Why? They don't make love to a camera. Some movie actors don't have the specialized training to work on a stage. Many actors cannot make a transition to voice-over. Why? Their voice separated from their body is not interesting enough to stand on its own. Some actors don't do well in commercials. They don't have the intensity to make a memorable character in just thirty seconds. Some actors who are very intense make great supporting actors, but because they are too much to watch for extended periods of time they never play leads. I've always been regarded as a great "second banana." (This means I don't get the lead in comedies, but the best supporting roles.) When you are first starting, you probably don't have any idea what your niche might be. But, once you find your niche, exploit it as best you can.

After reading this chapter, I'm sure you'll probably want to go out and run a few furlongs while you let it all digest. But speaking of exercise, let's move on to the next chapter.

CHAPTER SIXTEEN

I Could Have Been an Athlete...
(Factory Maintenance)

I love athletics. As a kid, I couldn't spend enough time playing or watching sports. Mr. Cub, Ernie Banks, was my hero. Number 14 roamed the friendly confines of Wrigley Field for my entire childhood. To this day, I consider myself lucky that I was able to watch this gifted man play baseball at the height of his career. WGN broadcast every Cub game. I used to run home from school just to see Ernie Banks bat in the last couple innings of the game. It was always worth the run to see Ernie hit one over the vine-covered walls of Wrigley. All in all, Ernie Banks hit 512 home runs, and I saw over half of them. Ernie's favorite expression was: "Let's play two today!" He loved to play doubleheaders because he got to play twice as much baseball. (Imagine one of today's players saying that!) It was obvious that he loved to play baseball. He worked hard at it, and he couldn't get enough of it. The last time I saw Ernie play I was in college. It was still a thrill to watch him bat.

But, as he ran down the line to first, everyone could see his legs were gone. He retired at the end of the season. It was hard to believe, but Ernie Banks had gotten old. As a kid, it didn't seem possible that that sort of thing could happen to someone. I always thought I would always be able to do whatever I wanted if I worked hard enough at it — but you can't. You get old and things that were easy become hard.

I'm not as famous as Ernie Banks, but I've got a favorite expression, too: "Don't squeeze the lemon until you want the juice." Actually, I heard a horse trainer use that expression just before the Preakness; he used the expression to describe his training schedule for the horse he was running in the race. Acting is a lot of work. You will feel squeezed many times during your career. Get used to sixteen-hour days in difficult conditions. Get used to thinking like a blue-collar worker because that is what you are about to become. Acting is physical work. If you doubt me, look the word up in the dictionary. To act is to do; to act is to perform; to act is hard physical work. Personally, I love to work as much as Ernie Banks loved to play baseball. Maybe I could coin a phrase like, "Let's do two shows today!"

I think I learned the most about acting in the first hour of the first acting class I took in college. Doctor Fred Sitton was teaching the class. I acted in many plays that Doc directed, and I will always remember what he said that first day: "Do it!" Those two simple words say everything there is to be said about what it takes to be a professional actor. If you can do it, you can act it; if you can't do it, they'll find someone else who can. You can study a part forever and know everything there is to know about a character, but if you physically cannot do the requirements of the part, you will not get the role. Sure they have stunt performers for certain things, but you need to be close to what they want to begin with. Stage actors are more in control of their work than film actors. But, in general,

I would say that acting is 10 percent intellectual and 90 percent physical. I've studied all the popular acting methods, and I know what it is like to study a part. But, when all is said and done, you can't talk about the character to an audience — you must do the character for the audience. No one sees what goes on inside your head while you are acting. All anyone ever reacts to is what they see and hear. Finding physical ways to make your ideas seen and heard is what acting is all about.

Maybe this will make you feel better. An actor is the most intellectual of all athletes. If you want to be a successful actor, you better know a lot about your body. Train it well and take care of it. It is all you have to earn a living with, and you only get one. I have been an athlete my entire life. I love to work out and play competitive games. I played baseball and softball for almost forty years. I played basketball competitively for many years. I was a gymnast in high school and was voted Mr. Physically Fit my senior year. As you already know, my parents wanted me to be a golf pro. I made the tennis team in high school. In my adult life, I have learned to run competitively in 10K races. I also played in a men's ice hockey league. I have taken dance classes for many years. I have learned to do a lot of physical things so that my body is ready to do whatever a director asks me to.

Perhaps I go overboard with exercise. You don't have to do as much as I have. But the better shape you are in, the better chance your career will have. If you have physical limitations, your opportunities will be diminished. Actors are vibrant, energetic people. They have stamina and enthusiasm. They willingly accept challenges. If you are going to be an actor, your motto should be, "mens sana in corpore sano." If your Latin is a bit rusty, that means it is desirable to have a sound mind inside a sound body. It sort of sounds like the description of class in thoroughbred horses, doesn't it?

At the very least, I suggest you plan on taking voice and

dance classes for the rest of your life. It doesn't matter that you might not plan on ever singing or dancing in your career. Those classes work every muscle you will ever need to use. Those classes will keep you limber and fit. Those classes will teach you where your limitations are. Three one-half-hour vocal workouts a week are adequate; three forty-five-minute dance/aerobic workouts are sufficient. Have a vocal coach available to you. If you don't want to go to dance or exercise classes, use videotapes. It is very easy to find an excuse not to do your exercises, but remember, you are running a business. You can't let your product look shabby. Sometimes, the boss has to move the lard off the loading dock himself. Be hard on yourself, it will pay off someday.

If you don't feel comfortable going to dance classes, find other activities to take their place. It doesn't matter which activities you choose. It could be snow shoveling or bowling. Just pick something you like so that you will stick with it. The only reason I recommend dance is that it combines everything you need to accomplish in one workout. It keeps you strong, agile, and limber while it continues to challenge you to learn new ways to move your body. Dancers think in terms of kinetics instead of words. I am continually amazed at the expressive movements dancers come up with. They always think of things I never consider. But, movement is their discipline. Likewise, my voice coach knows everything there is to know about the voice. He has taught me how to pull sounds out of my voice that I never thought possible. He has taught me how to take care of my voice when I have overused it during a show. He has helped me adjust my voice when I have fallen into bad habits. Just when I think I know everything, he teaches me something I have never considered. It really is a good idea to have someone that can evaluate you and give you a good objective opinion when you need it. Never stop training your body.

Why am I stressing the physical so much? You see lots of people in films who are overweight and seemingly out of shape. You're right. But, one thing I have discovered is that those people are in far better shape than anyone might imagine. Remember, you run your own business. It is up to you to decide how hard you want to work. You pick the jobs you want to do or don't want to do. I have been in good enough shape to do the jobs other actors did not want to do. An important part of my early career was doing difficult physical parts. Directors knew they could count on me to do complicated scenes involving action. Because it is expensive to shoot action scenes a director chooses an actor with a good reputation for that skill. I worked a lot with Joe Sedelmaier who is a famous commercial director known for amazing physical comedy. One time he asked me to do a beer commercial with him. (The head of the Northwestern Theater Department's prophesy was fulfilled!) He didn't audition me; he just gave me the job based on my ability to do physical comedy. Great, huh? When I got to the studio, a small restaurant set was built inside a small Ferris wheel. He explained to me that I was to play a waiter. All I had to do was walk from one wall of the set to the other. Simple, huh? But, of course, there was much more to it than that. Once I cleared the frame, I was to grab onto two handrails attached to the wall. As soon as I cleared, the Ferris wheel would rotate and I would end up on the ceiling of the set holding onto these two handrails for dear life until the take was over. Then they would rotate the Ferris wheel back to where it started. You are probably wondering why we did this. At the center of the set was a couple having an elegant dinner. Everything was glued into place on the set. The woman raised her beer glass and pointed it across the table at the man. He lifted the beer bottle and pointed it at her glass. The beer shot across the table and filled her glass. The man and woman were strapped into their chairs. When the man pointed the bottle, the Ferris wheel turned so that he was rotated to the ceiling. Gravity made the beer pour out of the bottle across the table into the glass. We did twenty-two takes of that shot. Never once did he miss the glass when he poured, and never once did I lose my grip and fall. The director hired people he knew could handle the job. This was complicated for a commercial. Imagine what being on a set for a Sylvester Stalone or Arnold Schwartzenegger film would be like!

I have been filmed outdoors on frozen lakes in weather below zero. I have had dynamite charges explode from my chest and stomach as I have been machine-gunned to death. Mr. T has thrown me through a door. I have driven high-speed, auto-chase sequences. I have been buried in potatoes until I was almost crushed by them. I have worked with broken bones, high fevers, and every type of flu known to man. During one period, I worked twenty-six 100-hour weeks in a row without a break. I've taken punches and pratfalls. I've been slapped so hard my teeth hurt. I've shot scenes in pig sties and flophouses. I've even done three shows a night in Cleveland! You never know what you will be asked to do. So it makes a lot of sense to be ready to do anything.

Be ready to do anything, but also learn to pace yourself: "Never squeeze the lemon until you want the juice." You need to be at your peak to be ready to perform. Save your body until you are ready to use it. If you are a theater actor, you have a regular regimen. You know when you are expected to perform each day. You can plan your stretches and warm-ups into your schedule. Whatever you do, don't skip them. I have learned the hard way. If you don't treat your body well, it will desert you. Muscles tear, hamstrings pull, and nodes develop. When you're young, injuries heal quickly. As you get older, you wish you had never had an injury. Injuries shorten a career and can mean unemployment. If you get sick or injured too often, you might develop a reputation that will cause producers to think twice about hiring you. The old expression that the show must go on is a truism. I have only missed one performance in my entire career; laryngitis left me speechless. Take care of yourself.

While I am on the subject of the body, I want to mention grooming and skin care. If you are a professional actor, remember people think you're cool enough to pay money to look at you. Grungy might be in, but make yourself a "cool" grungy. When people meet you, you can either be unforgettable or very forgettable. Think about your appearance. One model I knew was going through a rebellious stage. She had an attractive militant look that was popular at the time, but she had the hands of a bricklayer. When you met her, you couldn't help but notice her hands. People would shake hands with her and remember her hands. It may sound like a silly thing, but it was costing her work. I mentioned it to her. She thought about it. She looked at some photos of herself. That convinced her. Her hands were so rough-looking, you looked more at her hands than her face. The next day she had a manicurist take care of her hands, and she immediately started working more often. Since that day, I have never seen her hands look bad.

Little things make a big difference. Most actors are striking in some way. For me, my bushy mustache helped balance my bushy eyebrows. Early in my career, a director asked me to shave off my mustache for a job, so I did. When I showed up on the set, he took one look at me and said: "You know, without your mustache, you have no personality at all." Makeup put a false mustache on me. But, times change and people change. Actors sometimes grow into their characters. An actor who didn't do well in his fifties might age into the prototypical grandfather. Many kid actors outgrow their images and never find a new identity. When I was in my twenties, people thought I looked like I was thirty or forty. I was in great shape for a forty-year-old so I worked a lot. When I got to be forty, people thought I was younger than I really was. Staying in shape pays off.

One last note about your body. Take care of the skin on your face. Your face is what people look at the most unless you are on *Bay Watch*. The skin on your face is very delicate. Once you start to get bags under your eyes, it becomes more and more difficult to light you. Many actors eventually have operations to have this condition corrected. (Just so that you know, many actors have work done to enhance their image. Fat is injected into lips, breasts are enlarged or lifted. Noses are straightened or made smaller, etc., etc.) Early in my career, an older model told me that she kept her skin looking great through exercise and applying liquid Vitamin E to the skin under her eyes each night. I've done the same thing each night for my entire career, and it's worked for me. Makeup people like working on me because it is easy to make me look good. Lighting people always say it's easy to light me. I've always been grateful for that little tip, and I wanted to pass it on to you. Check with your doctor to be safe.

How I managed to move from Ernie Banks to skin care is beyond me, but everything in this last chapter made perfect sense to me. Acting is a physical job. The more you know about your instrument and the better you take care of it, the more performance you will get out of it. There are only so many squeezes in the lemon. Don't wear your body out foolishly. Exercise, eat right, and sleep well. Be rested and ready to work whenever you are called. You never know where you will be going or what you will be asked to do.

CHAPTER SEVENTEEN

I Could Have Been a Hollywood Agent...
(Managing a Sales Force)

Hey kid, I'm gonna make you a star!" How many times have you heard that line in old movies? It happens, but don't hang your star on it. To get involved in the business of acting, you are going to have to get involved with the business people of acting: talent agents. When you are just starting out, it will be very difficult to get an agent. The reason for this is very simple. Actors pay their agents 10 percent of what they earn. When your business is first starting, it is earning nothing. Ten percent of nothing is still nothing. Imagine owning a company that earns no money and expecting to attract an experienced, successful, wealthy salesman with excellent business contacts to work for you when you are offering him nothing. To compound the problem, you don't have a proven product, you don't have good advertising materials, and you're not even sure what your product line will be yet. Additionally, your competition is vying for the same sales representative's time and attention. Each year at the same time, thousands of actors graduate from schools and enter the profession. To get work, you need an agent; but to get an agent, you need to have worked. It is a very interesting Catch 22. Your first hurdle will be a difficult one to cross, but you'll need to find a way.

The most common way that actors get agents is through an "in." Someone you know makes a phone call or writes a letter for you. If you are an outstanding student at a prestigious school that is well-connected, that someone will probably be an instructor of yours. It might be a fellow actor who thinks enough of you to introduce you to his or her agent. Maybe your parents know someone. Your goal is to get your foot in the door. You have to sell a salesperson on the idea of selling you. It was just like my Fuller Brush man job. Once I found a way to get my foot in the front door, it was up to my natural charm and savior faire to close the deal.

If you do not have an "in," you are not alone. Very few fledgling actors are well-connected. I sure wasn't. I had one friend that had an agent. That agent met with me as a courtesy to my friend and wasn't overwhelmed by my natural charm and savior faire. My first meeting with an agent was much tougher than selling brushes door-to-door. As I sat in the meeting, working actors drifted in and out of this very busy agent's office. They all looked great and said things like: "Hi, Babe!" "You look incredible, darling." "Ciao!" (It was 1972.) Everybody was so comfortable it made me incredibly uncomfortable. I did not belong. A lot of these actors spent more money on their haircuts than I spent on my entire wardrobe. The agent asked to see my pictures. I pulled out a few pictures of me taken during stage shows from the second balcony. You could almost make out my face in a few of them. "These won't do," she said "You need a head shot." I was smart enough not to say I had a nice class picture taken when I graduated. She suggested I see a new photographer who was "fabulous"! That photographer was the only thing I had to cling to.

I left my first meeting with an agent in a completely despondent state. It was obvious this agent had a ton of stuff happening. Every actor in the place seemed rich and successful. I felt like a very poor second cousin. I was not in the same league as these actors. I was a successful theater actor from a small town in Indiana; these actors were successful television actors from Chicago. I had gone from being a big fish in a small pond to being a minnow in Lake Michigan. Think back to my chapter about thoroughbred racing. I was suddenly outclassed, and I felt acutely inferior. I felt like I had an overwhelming task ahead of me. I stood at the base of Mount Everest with a photographer's phone number in my hand.

But, I had come this far, and I didn't want to quit now. I called the photographer, and I got professional head shots. Before you see any agent, make sure you have a professional picture taken by a photographer who specializes in actor's head shots. Also make sure you have a résumé of your work in standard actor résumé form. Your first meeting will go a lot better than mine did. Meetings with agents will be significant to your career. Agents meet a lot of actors. They can't represent every one of them. They represent the ones they hit it off with. An agent wants to represent actors that represent themselves well. Learn to be a good conversationalist. When you meet an agent, have some things to talk about. Talk about things you've done. Talk about things you'd like to do. Give the agent an idea what your personal interests and hobbies are. Try to find a common ground so you can feel each other out. When you walk out of a meeting with an agent, that agent needs to feel comfortable with you and you have to feel comfortable with that agent.

Which brings us to a very interesting point. Just as there are different categories of actors, there are different categories of agents. There are agents who are very powerful and agents who are just barely getting by. You need to find the one who is right for you. The first agent I interviewed with had no interest in me, but one of her young agents did. I checked in with her twice a day for months before I got my first job — an extra on a Sears commercial. She sent me on that because she felt sorry for me and wanted to give me a break because I was trying so hard. Imagine what I thought when I went on that job and saw a lot of the people I saw in that agent's office the first day I met her. Many of the actors I thought were so successful were working as extras on a Sears commercial. After I established a strong reputation for myself as an actor, I was signed by a very powerful agent. Unfortunately this agent was not a good match for me because he had other clients who were more important. He didn't spend much time finding work for me because I was financially not worth the effort. He took me on as a long shot. I sat idle for weeks at a time and I made less money than when I was with a less powerful agent.

You need to find an agent who has an interest in you. Agencies that have the least work tend to be nicest to actors because they have the time to do it. Many very successful agencies limit registration and only take on actors when they lose one to another agency. Ideally, you want to get an agent who has contacts, time, and an interest in you. That sounds like a tall order, but it is an achievable objective. When you are starting out, your tendency will be to sign with anyone who is interested in you. Quite frankly, at that point in your career, you will be lucky to get anyone to be interested in you. Once you sign with an agent, it is important to realize that your relationship is a two-way street. Your agent will get you a large percentage of your opportunities, but it is just as important for you to bring opportunities into your agent's office. Your day will be spent out on the street trying to find work on your own. When you talk to other actors, you learn about what jobs are auditioning. No agent gets calls for every job that is auditioning. Tell your agent about job opportunities so they can follow up on them for you and other actors at your agency. Once a talent agency develops a star, it is amazing how many other opportunities develop for other actors at that agency. If you get in on the ground floor of an agency that is growing, your career will grow with it if you help develop the business for the agency. The power, strength, and prestige of an agency is directly dependent upon the actors it represents. As agencies lose important clients, their business declines; as agencies gain important clients, they grow. Some agencies grow too large and disintegrate. They don't have time to service all their actor clients' needs and they lose their business. I saw this happen twice in my career. The first agent I interviewed with held 60 percent of the business in Chicago in 1970; now that agent holds less than 3 percent. The agent I spent much of my career with grew from a small reputable agent to the largest, most-powerful agent in Chicago in about a ten-year period. Then, that agent starting losing key actors and that agency has declined to a diminished status. Other agencies have taken over. Just as actors' careers have ups and downs, so do agents' careers.

The relationship of agent and actor is incredibly complex. It is a relationship built upon trust, mutual respect, and planning. Both parties must have regular meetings. The actor must let the agent know what his goals and aspirations are. Do you want to do plays, commercials, movies, or what? The agent must let the actor know how realistic those goals are based upon performance and feedback. The worst thing that can happen in the relationship is that communications cease. When people stop talking, everybody stops making money. Twice in my career, an agent got bad feedback about one of my auditions. In both cases, the agent didn't tell me about the feedback until I asked. In both cases, my agent stopped sending me out on auditions for extended periods of time. In the first instance, I was just starting out. I was not important to the agent, and he didn't care if he lost me. It taught me the business can be cruel and unfeeling. In the second instance, I was a well-established actor earning a lot of money for an agent. It was easier for that agent to collect fees on work I was bringing into the agency than talk about the audition. I dissolved my relationship with that agent. Since that agent lost confidence in me, it was time to move on. Why pay someone who is no longer interested in working for you? We parted on friendly terms. In both cases, communication breakdowns resulted in a failed business relationship. One hurt me; one hurt an agent. In both cases, it was not good business.

Remember, only one person is going to be responsible for finding you work — you! Don't expect an agent or a manager to make your career the only thing they think about. You are responsible for you. An agent is only a portion of your sales force. Ultimately, you will be the driving force behind your career. If someone comes along and makes you a star, great! But don't hold your breath. Remember, an agent represents many people. If someone makes more money for an agent than you do, that actor will be most likely to get the major portion of your agent's attention. If you want the attention, do the work it takes to stimulate the attention — find work on your own. If you want water, prime the pump!

CHAPTER EIGHTEEN

I Could Have Been a Teamster...
(Dealing with Unions)

ctors are artists. They think lofty thoughts. They walk
through life with a calm self-assurance. They are
important. Audiences sit and watch in rapture as they
perform their magic. They sip champagne at chichi opening
night parties. All actors share a deep emotional bond forged
through shared experiences in their art and craft. But, did you
know that all professional actors are members of the AFL-
CIO? The major actor unions — SAG (Screen Actors Guild),
AFTRA (American Federation of Television and Radio
Artists), and AEA (Actor's Equity Association) — are all part
of the AFL-CIO. If you plan on being a professional actor, plan
on joining these organizations.

SAG is the union for work that you do on film. It doesn't
matter what the work is. You can shoot motion pictures, television shows, industrial films, or commercials on film. If the
project is shot on film, it is a SAG job. If the job is shot on

videotape or goes out live on radio or television, it is AFTRA. This may sound very simple, and once upon a time, it was. But the introduction of digital technology has blurred the distinction between AFTRA and SAG. Many projects are no longer filmed or taped, but they are recorded digitally. The unions are still struggling to define which union claims the new technology. But if you plan on being a professional actor, you'll need to join both unions. SAG is primarily composed of actors. AFTRA, however, is composed of actors, broadcasters, and newscasters. AEA is the union for stage actors. It is the smallest of the three major unions. The work done under AEA is primarily theater and industrial shows. There is a fourth union that some actors belong to. It is called AGVA (American Guild of Variety Artists), but odds are you'll never join that union unless your career is centered in Las Vegas, Atlantic City, or Bramson, Missouri, performing in revues. AGVA is mostly for specialty acts like magicians or chorus dancers.

Why are there so many unions for actors? As we have established, most actors are not trained to think like business people. In 1999, AFTRA and SAG members voted on a merger of the two unions. The merger has been under discussion for the past thirty years. AFTRA members voted for the merger, but the Los Angeles members of SAG worked hard to defeat it. They wanted to preserve the elite image of the SAG union. As a result, actors continue to pay for two sets of union offices, contract negotiations, dues, initiation fees, and expenses. In union dues, it costs more than ever before to be an actor, and fewer actors will probably qualify for health and welfare benefits. AFTRA and SAG continue to bargain collectively for actors to gain equal contracts where their work overlaps. If none of this makes sense to you, you're not alone. Hope springs eternal that the acting unions will merge to eliminate duplicate levels of bureaucracy, administration expenses, and waste, but until then you will need to plan on joining all three unions if you intend to become a professional actor. So let me explain in detail what is involved when you join the unions.

How much do you know about President Taft? You'll hear his name a lot when you are starting out. "Have you Taft-Hartleyed yet?" That phrase is probably the only thing most actors have to thank President Taft for. It is expensive to join actors' unions. Have at least $3,000 in cash set aside to join these organizations. They don't accept checks. After all, you're an out-of-work actor. It costs $800 to join Actor's Equity, $1,258 to join AFTRA, and $1,322 to join SAG. You probably won't have to join all three at once, but you never know. Thanks to the Taft-Hartley act, you can work for one month under each of these unions before you will be asked to join. You get to Taft-Hartley once in your life for each of the three unions. They keep very good records of who has Taft-Hartleyed for each union. So even if you signed thirty years ago, they know all about it.

How do you get to join the union? Agents can put new actors on SAG and AFTRA auditions. All you need to do is win the audition. AEA is a little different. They try to protect their members by limiting auditions to members only. Every once in a while, they schedule a few audition times for non-union talent. AEA also allows a certain number of actors who are nonunion to work with union members under the Equity Membership Candidacy Program. After fifty-five weeks of employment under this program, you can join Actor's Equity. You still have to pay the membership fee, though. If you want to be a professional and compete at the highest levels, you need to join the unions. If you want to do this as a career, you need to join the unions. The business is organized around obtaining talent from union-franchised agents. So if you want to act professionally, plan on joining the unions.

There are about 39,000 members in Actor's Equity Association, 99,000 members in SAG, 63,000 members in

AFTRA, and 5,000 members in AGVA. In total there are about 206,000 memberships. However, remember that most people belong to more than one union. The unions do not keep cross-reference charts of members who belong to the other unions, but I would guess that there are about 100,000 actors included in these memberships at any given time. In addition, there are many more actors trying to get into the unions. Since those people are unaffiliated, there is no way to know how many of them there are. If I were to hazard a guess, I would estimate that there are probably about 125,000 people seeking acting work at any given time. About 15 percent of the members in any of the unions make full-time salaries in that union. However, the number of people making full-time livings is higher when you add their earnings together for all the unions. For example, a stage actor might make $15,000 in AEA and $2,500 each in AFTRA and SAG. That would mean that the actor would come up as a successful actor in one union and as a part-timer in the other two. In reality, two of the unions only augment that actor's income for his primary work. This is a pretty typical scenario for most beginning actors. Young actors start in theater because that is what they did in college. Eventually actors need to make money in SAG and AFTRA, too. The jobs in those unions is where the big dollars are because the work eventually creates residual income. In general, Actor's Equity and AGVA hourly wages are low compared to AFTRA and SAG wages. As you are starting your business, you'll need to determine how much effort you will want to invest in finding work in each of the unions.

Remember, you are going to be running your own business. In most instances that would mean you are self-employed. However, in most instances, the union has worked it out that you are regarded as an employee. This may seem like a bunch of legal gobbledygook, but if you are going to run a successful business you need to know what the difference is between being self-employed and being an employee. It will make a big difference to your bottom line. If someone hires you for an acting job and you make over $600.00, they are required to withhold taxes and pay the employer side of social security benefits since you are, by law, considered an employee. However, many employers still argue that you are an independent contractor and should pay your own benefits. I have known many actors who were shocked when the IRS came after them. For example, one actor I know was paid $30,000 ($600 a week) by one company. He lived like he was making $600 a week. When tax time came, he owed $5,000 in federal tax, $900 in state tax, $2,400 in social security and $2,400 in self-employment tax. This was a very painful lesson. He didn't have the money so he had to pay penalties to the I.R.S., which cost him more money! To make matters worse, since he didn't keep his receipts for road expenses, he couldn't write off his expenses against his income. That cost him more money. The company had him sign a letter stating that he was an independent contractor and was responsible for his own taxes, so he didn't have a leg to stand on. Some employers will consider you self-employed. If you accept the work as an independent contractor, remember that a big portion of your check will go to the government and state; you will also be responsible for having an accountant do your paperwork for taxes on a timely basis.

Many actors form corporations for their business dealings. This allows them to consider themselves independent contractors who are self-employed. For most actors, this will cost you more money than it is worth. Do a lot of research before you incorporate. Most accountants and attorneys do not completely understand the business of acting. It is a very unique profession. There can be advantages to this approach, but not until you are making a lot of money. If you are making several hundred thousand dollars a year, you might want to incorporate and pay self-employment tax. The only really big advantage of being incorporated is that some companies prefer to hire actors who are corporations to avoid employer-side contributions to social security and possible unemployment claims. But don't begin your career as a corporation. You'll have much more pressing financial needs when you are starting out.

The labor unions consider you an employee (but if you want to be a successful business person, remember that you are your own boss) because there are many advantages for the average actor. First of all, you don't have to retain an accountant to file your weekly and monthly taxes. Secondly, you don't have to pay self-employment tax (your employers incur that expense). Thirdly, you can collect unemployment benefits. Unfortunately there is a downside to being an employee: You don't get to deduct as many business expenses. But there is a way to take advantage of this situation. Some actors split their income into independent contractor jobs (no taxes withheld) and employee jobs (taxes withheld). To compensate for the taxes that aren't withheld on your independent contractor jobs, you can request your other employers to withhold extra taxes. By withholding more than necessary, your employers who withhold taxes are covering most of your taxes that weren't withheld on the jobs you did as an independent contractor. This strategy has worked well for me over the years. Check with your accountant to to see if this will work well for you.

Being part of a union gives you some other advantages. Most importantly the unions provide you with health insurance, hospitalization, and dental benefits. They will even provide these benefits for your family. These are provided at no cost to you, providing that you make enough money doing union work. The amounts of coverage vary with each union.

Additionally, the unions all have retirement funds. To be vested in any of the pension plans, you need to make qualifying amounts of income for ten years. (In AFTRA and AEA they can be in any ten years, but in SAG your ten years must occur in succession. This makes it very hard to gain full vesting in SAG.) If you have a thirty- or forty-year career, you can plan on having a very nice retirement income. Also, the unions provide you with life insurance. The amounts are small for each union, but at least your family will have something if anything ever happens to you. When you begin your career, things like health insurance, pension income, and life insurance might not seem important, but as you approach the end of your career, they become very important. People who have regular jobs get these benefits from their employers. Why should actors be any different than anyone else? Actors need all the things regular people need. The unions have worked hard to obtain health and insurance plans for members.

Another major advantage of being a union member is that the unions negotiate all the basic contracts you will work under. There are literally libraries of contracts for the unions. While you will probably not work under all the contracts, it's a good idea to know about the contracts you will be working under most frequently. If you are going to be in business, you should know what you will be signing. The hourly rates for most contracts are very high dollar amounts. Your time is worth money when you are working. Your agent will generally negotiate your overscale contracts, but even then it is a good idea to know about things like overtime so you can be paid correctly.

The unions are negotiating contracts all the time. Sometimes, the negotiating goes smoothly, but sometimes it doesn't. When it doesn't, you might find yourself walking up and down the street in front of a big company's building as a demonstrator for your union. When you are a union member, you walk picket lines. No one is excused from picket duty. The times I had to do it, I felt very out of place. I was an artist, not a teamster. But, I still did it. Don't ever forget that as an actor, you are a member of the AFL-CIO just like me and Julia Roberts. Your business will be affected by strikes and labor talks. They always seem to come at inconvenient times, but you'll learn to deal with that.

The year 2000 saw the longest strike in the history of the actor's unions. The strike involved our radio and television commercial contracts. The strike lasted six months and was our greatest test as a union. The controversy revolved around television commercial residuals. Changing technology has created many new outlets for commercials. The union commercial contracts were originally created for three major networks and local affiliates; in recent years, the market grew to also include hundreds of cable outlets as well as the Internet. The fight was long and bitter, but in the end, we retained our residual income structure and expanded our markets into cable and the Internet. The strike of 2000 was a battle for survival, and an actor's ability to make a liveable income was at stake. I never thought I would have to get as deeply involved with a labor strike as I did with this one, but it took the efforts of all to win. Fortunately, many of the other AFL-CIO unions came to our aid and helped us through the difficult times. Truck drivers refused to cross our picket lines and make deliveries. Other union workers joined our picket lines. Major stars like Paul Newman, Susan Sarandon, Alec Baldwin, and Richard Dreyfus were on the front lines with the rest of us. Our fight was against giant corporations, advertising agencies, and the networks. I think all actors learned that we can't take our income for granted in the future. The unions make a big difference in the business of acting.

During the strike, many nonunion and foreign actors took our jobs. We learned that we could be replaced for awhile. But the strike finally ended because we refused to buckle, and producers realized that the quality of the nonunion actors was not good enough for the long haul. As painful as it was to go through a prolonged strike, some good came out of it. It increased union actors' awareness of the importance our unions. If acting is to remain a profession, it must have organizations that fight for standards of just compensation. Acting is not all fun and games. Sometimes it is business in the most serious sense.

There are advantages and disadvantages to belonging to the unions, but the advantages far outweigh the disadvantages in the long run. If you want to become a professional actor, you'll need to join the union. When you first start out, you will probably get some paid nonunion work to get you going. But there is no future in this type of work. It gives you a short-term buck and experience, but there will be no residuals and no health or pension benefits. You will also be doing the lowest levels of professional work — but you have to start somewhere. Store-front theaters and local cable are good ways to build a résumé. But you will tire of it after awhile because you cannot go any higher or do any better quality work until you join the union. Be prepared when your chance comes. It will be difficult and expensive to make the jump, but necessary if you want to make acting a profession.

In recent years, the unions have been given considerable competition by foreign performers, nonunion performers, and a class of former union performers that are labeled "financial core." First of all, you need to know that SAG and AFTRA contracts extend outside the boundaries of the United States. There are many members in AFTRA and SAG who are noncitizens. However, U.S. actors are not allowed to join many of the foreign unions. For example, the Canadian Actors Union, ACTRA, is for Canadians only. To join, you must renounce your citizenship and become a Canadian. American actors are generally not allowed to work in Canada. It takes special clearance to get a work permit in Canada. Generally you have to have status as a celebrity who is internationally recognized. Because my work won the Cannes Film Festival, I achieved that status. But even though I had twenty years of benefits paid into ACTRA, I receive no benefits because I am not allowed to join the Canadian union.

I've already discussed nonunion workers in the United States. During each union strike, these performers cross union picket lines to do union work at a lower price. AFTRA/SAG members label these performers as "scabs" and ostracize them. During strikes, the unions announce they will not allow these people to join the union at a later date, but as best as I can tell, some of them eventually get to join the union. It is not a good idea to put yourself in this type of situation, because the members of your profession will look down upon you. It will taint your image in the performance community. When you cross the picket line, you hurt the future economic picture for all actors by creating a low-priced alternative. But the low-priced alternative always exists in right-to-work states. In those states, you do not have to use union labor. Texas, Georgia, and Florida are particularly hard states to earn a living in as a union actor. National advertisers in those states tend to use union talent, but the majority of the smaller jobs go to nonunion actors. Talent in those states can work for less than union rates, but very few if any of those performers have careers. They reduce acting to a hobby or sideline rather than a profession.

The final and most difficult source of competition for union members has come from within the rank and file members of the union. Thanks to a Supreme Court ruling, union members can resign their membership status and declare "financial core." These actors are allowed to do both union and nonunion work in exchange for giving up their union membership, voting privileges, and certain benefits. It has resulted in a group of performers who are slowly building up their businesses by undercutting union rates. There is a growing animosity among union members toward these performers.

One final world about joining the unions — do it. Without the unions, there would be no set standards for the business. Fair wages and working conditions would not be defined. Without the unions, there is no organized way to find actors. Without unions, actors would not have insurances or pension plans. Without unions the business of acting would not have a financial structure. Without unions, we would be roving bands of gypsies trying to scratch out what we can (many people still think of actors in this way anyway). If you want to be a professional actor with a future and a career, the unions need to be part of your business plan. You'll learn to live with the politics and, eventually, you'll learn to write off your dues as just another business expense.

CHAPTER NINETEEN

I Could Have Been a Banker...
(Financial Matters)

After I had been a professional actor for about eleven years, I was doing pretty well financially. We had already been home owners for ten years and were ready to expand into a larger house. We had an excellent credit record and could easily afford a more upscale home. My previous year's income was three times more than it needed to be to qualify for the mortgage on the home we wanted. Selling our current home allowed us to put almost 50 percent down on the house we were bidding on so we were excellent candidates for any bank's mortgage department. Imagine my surprise when the mortgage broker got back to us. "Mr. Cerny, good news! I found a bank that is willing to take a chance on you. They'll give you a loan for $5,000 more than your current mortgage." I sat in shocked silence. The bank essentially said if I sold my house, I could buy a house of the same value. I had almost completely paid off my previous mortgage and never missed a payment. In fact, we paid extra most months to get the loan down faster. "What's going on?" I asked. The broker looked at me and said, "You're an actor! You're lucky a bank is willing to talk with you at all. The bank wants to know what you really do for a living!"

The acting profession is filled with people who make poor business decisions. Bankers rate actors as one of the highest risk categories no matter how much money they make. No matter what our credit reports said, the computers picked up my "Occupation: Actor" status on the credit report and rejected it. At this point, I walked into the bank with a copy of *Ainsle's Complete Guide to Thoroughbred Racing* and proceeded to explain the differences between actors. That banker wasn't interested, so I took my excellent credit rating elsewhere and found a banker who was. When I explained the business of acting to him, he was quite impressed. I explained how 90 percent of my income was residual based. Once he understood that, it was apparent to him that I had a more stable job than he did. At the time, I had twenty-six commercials paying me residuals for extended periods of time; all he had as security was a two-week notice. I looked really good to him. However, normal lines of mortgages were closed to me at his bank, too, because I said the dirty word: actor! So, he let me borrow the money as a business loan based upon my business record. I promised him that I would pay the loan off in five years. I paid it off in fifty months (four years, two months). Everyone at the bank was impressed by my business acumen (no small wonder considering my accounting talent), and I have never had trouble getting a business loan ever since. You may not have as deep an interest in money as I do, but if you intend to run a successful business, it is a good idea to store these thoughts in the back of your mind. I had no one to guide me through these matters. I had to learn these things on my own. It was difficult as I learned by trial and error, but it made a difference in my acting career. Dealing with money matters taught me how to create a financially stable future for myself. The more money I had, the longer I could stay in business.

It is hard for an actor to get his or her business off the ground. Most actors fail to get their first job. They try to find work for a few months and get discouraged when they don't find it. In reality, it is going to take six months of really hard work before you can reasonably expect to get your first job. Most businesses are much easier to get off the ground. It is not like opening a store where customers walk in off the street and buy things. The business of acting is very special unto itself. It is very difficult to start a business when your only assets are your winning personality, your special look, and a pleasant voice. To get started, your only investor will be yourself. You will need to be your banker. You will need to be your financial advisor. Learn to be very hard on yourself because your first lesson must be frugality.

When I was at Northwestern, I enrolled in a course about silent film. I always loved Laurel and Hardy, Mabel Normand, Marie Dressler, Charlie Chase, and many of the silent film stars. Because I didn't know as much about Charlie Chaplin as the others I decided to read his autobiography. Charlie Chaplin's ability to deal with money was inspirational. He really knew the value of a dollar. He didn't become one of the most financially successful stars ever without knowing about money. Charlie Chaplin made himself a successful star. No one did it for him. He saved his money and reinvested it into his business. He knew how to make money, and it made a big difference in his career. He didn't like working for the big studios and having them make the big bucks. So, to eliminate the middleman, Charlie Chaplin, Douglas Fairbanks, and Mary Pickford formed United Artists! This goes way beyond Mickey and Judy doing a show in the barn. This amazing fact has stuck with me my whole career. What a great way to make art — unite a group of artists and let them work for themselves. This was a demonstration of resourcefulness and creativity that was unique in the business. Necessity is the mother of invention, and many theater companies have started the same way. The famous Steppenwolfe Theater Company started in very much the same manner. John Malkovich, John Mahoney, and Gary Sinise were notable founding members of Steppenwolfe. They started out in the basement of the Catholic Church in Highland Park, Illinois. Today, the Steppenwolfe Theater is in the heart of Chicago's theater district with a specially built state-of- the art theater. Most of the original founding members return with regularity to appear in the company's productions and ensure the future of the ensemble for other actors. The Second City was started by a group of students at the University of Chicago. That company is nearly fifty years old and has been a major stepping stone for over 300 stars. Resourceful actors learn to create employment for themselves and their friends. If you can't find work from others, make it yourself.

You may not plan on owning a major motion picture company or establishing a major theater company, but you need to understand how Charlie Chaplin's success relates to your circumstances. Charlie Chaplin started with nothing and ended up with fabulous wealth. In his autobiography, Chaplin goes into great detail about each dime that he made early in his career. He knew all the details about each deal he made. He didn't talk about art without talking about business. Considering he was one of the greatest actors of all time, that should tell you something. A steady stream of profits and ready financing meant a solid bankable business. Profitability was one of Chaplin's goals, and it has always been one of my goals, too. If you want to be around for awhile, it should be one of your goals, too.

There is an expression you will hear over and over again

in the business: "It's either feast or famine." Either there is way too much work or not enough. It is hard to believe, but sometimes one audition can generate a huge amount of money. If you win one national commercial, you might make ten to forty thousand dollars on that one day's work. That represents three years of theater work for most actors. How you manage windfall profits will mean a lot to your career. Most actors have gone without for long periods of time. When they get their hands on a large amount of money, they often spend it in lavish, unnecessary ways. They will take vacations or buy things they don't need. Learn to be frugal. Make your cash work for you. Invest wisely in your career. Set aside money for advertising and promotions to build your business. You need to make tapes, shoot new pictures, and have a reasonable wardrobe for interviews and auditions. You need money for union dues. As I've told you, you need to save money for a rainy day. The more money you have saved up, the more rainy days you can weather. You might go months at a time without winning a job, so you must have enough savings to remain available for auditions. There were times my savings dwindled down to a few hundred dollars, but I always found a way to keep my business solvent. Chaplin was always acutely aware of his financial condition, and I patterned my thinking on his frugal example. Believe me, many years I went without things to keep my business going. My wife and I didn't get to go on vacations for the first ten years we were married. We postponed having a family. We lived well below our means until my career flourished. It takes time to build a business, and money buys you time. The longer you stay in business, the better able you will be to find new ways to generate more work.

Most actors are used to living hand-to-mouth. It is difficult to imagine any other way after a while. But you need to think about things that will stabilize your future. Find a way to save money and then put that money into things that will build an asset base for you. Buy a house or two-flat as soon as you can; don't waste money on rent. Own something that will potentially bring in rental money for you so that you can supplement your income. Real estate appreciates. Make other investments that will appreciate for you, too. I learned to invest in the stock market and didn't touch my investments for years. They grew at a rate of about 15 percent a year. After a while, I was able to use that as collateral to get loans when I needed them. Whole-life insurance is also a good investment if you have a family. All these things can bring stability to a career. The vast majority of working actors in SAG, AFTRA, and AEA have families and homes. They have learned to take the things I have mentioned seriously. They don't live their lives out of suitcases; they go to work in the morning and go home at night. Producers hire them for the big jobs because they know they'll be there tomorrow, next week, and next year. They are not part-timers who drive cabs and wait tables. They are professional actors. Their full-time occupation is their business, and they are in business to stay.

I truly believe that having a home and a family made me a better actor. It forced me to find new business opportunities. I worked very hard for everything I have, and I value the things I have earned. I learned to make sensible financial decisions for my business because I had a house to pay for and a family to support. My early meetings with bankers angered me because I was not treated as well as any other person who worked hard for a living. The acting profession is filled with people who have a poor record with money matters. Bankers don't like to give loans to actors because the vast majority of actors eventually fail financially and call it quits. But I think there is a difference between being an actor and being a professional actor. If you want to be a professional actor, study money. It takes money to make money, but more importantly, it takes money to keep making more money. Get to know a banker on a first-name basis. Develop a relationship; it might come in handy some day. Computers will say you are a bad risk but finding a friendly ear can help make a difference. You don't need to live the life of a gypsy. Work toward developing a record of financial stability and your career will prosper.

CHAPTER TWENTY

I Could Have Been a Statistician...

(Evaluating Growth and Planning Expansion)

By now, you are probably getting the impression that I am a deadly dull, serious guy. Is it possible that this guy who has been on television all these years making millions of people laugh has the soul of an accountant? I have compared you to a horse, told you that you are a bad business risk, explained that your talent is not any greater than anyone else's, and thrown a wet blanket over every burning desire you have ever kindled. Acting is fun; this stuff is. . . stuff that my parents always talked about. OK, let's take a break and talk about theater! Willie Loman. *Death of a Salesman.* Who can't relate to this tragic story? It's the great American play! Every actor wants to play Willie or Linda. Why? Because it is a play about business? Because it is a play about life and death? Why didn't Willie see the handwriting on the wall? Why didn't he

get a job doing something else? He could have been a cabdriver
. . . actually, he couldn't have been a cabdriver! That was the
whole point, wasn't it? He couldn't be what he was, so he
couldn't be at all. How sad, how tragic, I'm picking on Willie
Loman! See I do have a sense of humor, and I'm fun to be with
after all.

I wasn't sure whether to title this chapter "statistician" or
"journalist." You need to keep a journal, but your journal is
mostly statistics. I don't think Willie kept his sales journal as
well in his later years as he did in his early years. Boy, did he
pay the price! You will have no way of knowing if your business is growing or dying until you start making year-to-year
comparisons. The members of my voice group, These People
Talk Funny, occasionally get together to compare "body
counts" as we call them. "Body counts" are the number of
commercials and auditions we have during a year. We compare
them to the previous year and determine if each of us is keeping pace with the rest of the business. If we are all up or down
about the same amount, it is a sign of a good year or bad year.
If everyone is up and one person is down, we have uncovered
a personal problem. This sort of information can help you figure out what you need to do to help your business. You can do
the same sort of comparisons my group does with your
friends. Even when I was with The Second City, we used to get
together to compare notes. If you can compare notes with a
group of friends, it will help you. If you can't, at least plan on
compiling year-end results and comparing your own work
from year to year.

Depending on what you are doing, there are many statistics that will help you create a future business plan. First of all,
figure out how your work is divided between the unions. Then
break it down into other categories. What percentage of your
work is theater, film, television, commercials, industrial films,
and so forth? What percentage of your work do you find and

what percentage does your agent find? Twice in my career I discovered that I was paying my agent more in agent fees than my agent was finding in work for me; both times I dissolved the relationship with the agent when my contract was up. How much work do your promotional materials generate? Should you re-evaluate the expenditure? How much money do you spend on your car, cabs, and public transportation? How much money do you spend on travel to find work in other cities? Is it worth extended trips to New York and Los Angeles? How much money are you spending on continuing education? Sometimes it is good to change coaches and teachers and learn a new technique. Improv classes might be more productive for you than method classes. A sports activity might give your workout program a new slant.

Statistics tell you what is happening in your career. Take time to compile them. Take time to study them. Every good businessperson does. Auto manufacturers change their product line each year. They send out endless questionnaires in the mail asking customers to evaluate their product. They study the results and produce new products based upon what they find. As an actor you will also be changing. You will get older. You will look different. With experience, you will get better at certain things. With age your physical skills will diminish and eventually you might not be able to perform at the level you used to. Your product will change with time and with the times. Don't allow yourself to get too comfortable with your product. Continuously adjust the product you are selling. The only way to tell if people are satisfied with the product they are buying is to look at statistics. Statistics will tell you if you are maintaining a level of work in a certain area or if it is starting to decline. Statistics will tell you if a new area of work is generating more income than an old one. When changes like these happen, you need to consider your options.

From time to time, go back and look at old pictures of

yourself. Listen to old tapes of yourself. Watch old videos of yourself. See if your current image of yourself matches what you see in the mirror or in the old pictures and tapes. Make note of changes you see and hear. There is nothing worse than being out of style. Statistics always tell the truth. If you are frequently losing a type of audition you used to win, find out the reason why. Have you grown too old? Has your image not changed with the times? Are people tired of seeing you in that part? Looking at work that you have done from many years past will prove this point. You will laugh at some of your old work. Some of it you will discover is better than you remembered. But one thing is for sure — you will notice that you have changed significantly. You're not Peter Pan and you don't live in never-neverland. As with any successful business, you need to use statistics to evaluate success and failure. Ignorance is never bliss when you suddenly find yourself out of business. The business of acting should not be thought of as a lucky streak that can come to an end at any time; acting is a career that requires planned progress. Willie Loman lived in the past. He climbed to a plateau and never wanted to go any higher. When you become satisfied with the status quo, your acting career will begin to stagnate and die. Acting is about communication. If your style of communication is not fresh and timely, chances are you will not be as attractive to producers. Don't become Willie Loman unless Arthur Miller is involved!

CHAPTER TWENTY-ONE

I Could Have Been a Pain in the Butt...
(Managing Success)

Have you ever gone into a store where the salesperson was doing so well that he did not want to sell you anything? "Can I have a six boxes of macaroni and cheese and a pound of hamburger?" (a typical beginning actor's shopping list). The grocer snurls up his nose and says: "No. I don't feel like it. I sold all the groceries I need to sell today. Come back tomorrow; maybe I'll need to sell something then." After you get your first television series, you walk into your local Ferrari dealership and ask to buy the shiny red car in the window. The Ferrari salesman says: "I don't care how much money you have, that car is staying in my showroom window. I don't need to sell a Ferrari today." The first example is theater of the absurd; the second example is elite snobbism. All actors can become enchanted by both. I cannot tell you how many actors I have seen ruin their careers by letting their inflated egos and satiated bank accounts get the best of their common sense.

It is very hard to find acting work. It is much easier to lose it. As I have mentioned, every actor's primary activity is looking for work. Doing the work is a pleasure; finding the work is arduous. We have discussed the feast-and-famine principle from a practical financial standpoint but not from a psychological standpoint. Success is very difficult to come by, but when it does come, your world can be suddenly turned upside down. Everyone wants you. Money pours in. You have multiple offers. Many actors don't know how to respond to lavish attention if they've never had it. Believe it or not, many actors become abusive and start to play hard to get. We all know the story about the grasshopper who fiddles away his days in the sun; one day the weather turns cold, and he's the insect version of Willie Loman (a potential series pilot if I ever heard one). An actor who has gone from hand-to-mouth for many years suddenly has a good run and makes a windfall of $20,000. Suddenly he is on easy street. Even more suddenly he becomes a walking liability to his career. "I'm going on vacation!" "Talk to my agent, we're not really interested in industrial videos right now. We're looking for television series work." "Do a commercial? I'm consumed doing a meaningful play in a waiver house (i.e., no pay)." "It takes a little more money than that to get me interested in projects like yours these days." "Been there, done that, had it, no need to repeat it." These are all things I've heard actors say after obtaining a small measure of success.

Success kills so many careers. One actor I know was doing all the announcing for a major beer company. He had done it for years and was making a ton of money. He was in a bar near the advertising agency that did the commercials that were making him rich. Two men asked him if he wasn't the famous TV announcer that did the beer commercials. He said he was.

When the men asked him why he wasn't drinking the beer he advertised on television, he responded, "I wouldn't drink that shit if you paid me." Was it a prudent move to say something like this in public? There is no doubt he let his ego and bravado get the best of him. The two men turned out to be brewery executives for the beer he did the announcing for. The next morning all his commercials were pulled off the air, and he was replaced permanently. The star of a television series I was working on was very vocal on set about how stupid the show was. She hated working in Chicago; she couldn't wait to get back to L.A. so she could relax. The writers were all idiots. Imagine how the cast and crew surrounding her felt. It was like being on the *Titanic*. No one wanted to work hard to save the series because the star was more interested in going home and playing than working hard. Needless to say the series was canceled and the "star" became a thirteen-week wonder who never had a second series. Before the series she had good series and movie roles and a future. Word of her attitude toward "her" series spread quickly to the studios and other networks. Overnight, she gained a bad reputation that put a screeching halt to her career.

Actors like these are royal pains in the butt. They require inordinate amounts of attention and stroking. They complain and make life miserable for everyone around them. As silly as this may sound, we even encounter these type of actors in local community theaters. "I'm only doing the show because the theater would collapse without my magnificent talent!" "I'm so busy, I don't know why I'm doing this!" These people are called prima donnas. Don't ever let yourself become one because it will be the end of you. When successful actors get together, they always complain about how many hours it took to do this job or that job. They complain about how long a certain casting director always makes them wait. They complain about salaries; "Who wants to work for $500 a day?"

The business is filled with whiners and complainers. Actors who used to complain about not working enough, suddenly start to complain about working too much. If you do too much complaining around the wrong people, you will kill your career.

It takes a big ego to become an actor. You have to believe in yourself. You have to believe you are a thoroughbred. You have to sell yourself. You have to keep yourself pumped up. It is important to do these things to keep yourself going. BUT NEVER BELIEVE YOUR OWN PROPAGANDA. Stay humble. Be grateful. Every night thank your lucky stars that you are a working actor. Remember how hard it was to find work when you first started out. You are replaceable, and every actor you've ever auditioned against is waiting for you to screw up. There are enough factors working against you without you working against yourself. Don't be self-destructive. If you stop and think about the examples I've given, I'm sure you can find similar examples from watching actors around you. I find myself complaining from time to time. But you need to develop a very different frame of mind. At an audition one actor asked one of the most successful actors I know why he was at the audition. "With all the stuff you've got on the air, why are you auditioning?" The successful actor looked the other actor right in the eye and said: "Because I want to win this audition. I want to win every audition. I want to do every job. There is no such thing as too much work or too much money." I never met a successful business person who didn't say exactly the same thing. When you go into a store, they want you to buy more so they can sell more. The acting business is the same way. Don't shoot yourself in the foot and drive work away by making people think you're too successful, too busy, or too disinterested to want to work. Let people know that you enjoy what you do and that you can't wait to do more of it. Be a joy to work with; don't be a pain in the butt!

Remember that each actor is only a small part of a production. Actors that gain a reputation as being difficult to work with soon find themselves out of work. Actors need to be the most responsible people on Earth if they expect to have careers. When actors work, they start when they start and they finish when they finish. Acting is not a nine-to-five job. Always arrive at the job early and never allow yourself to be late. Time is money. Production is the ultimate team activity. If you are involved in principal photography, probably fifteen people will be hard at work three hours before you arrive in an effort to make you look good. No one will think it's funny that you overslept. It works differently with a play. If you are late for a rehearsal, most directors simply take you out in back of the theater and shoot you. Arriving late is strictly forbidden.

When you are the center of attention on a job, be nice to everybody. Make everyone's job easy. If the lighting person asks you to stand in, do it. Don't give the costumer and make-up person trouble. Don't play with the props and break them. If you're having a bad day, don't take it out on the people around you. Because you are an actor, people will treat you like you are special. Don't take advantage of it. Act like you are special and be nice to the people around you. All the things I am mentioning may seem like common sense, but I have seen incredibly rude behavior from actors that I have never seen from any other group of people. Even if it is absolutely true that you are important and the center of attention at every job you do, that doesn't mean you are the only one that matters. You will be treated like royalty, but you are not! Don't act uppity! You can be replaced in the bat of an eyelash. Everybody else involved in a production is just as important as you are. On a movie set, people will fuss over the camera just as much as you. Don't cause any more problems than the camera does.

One time an actor made someone drive across town in the

middle of a shoot because the bottled water came from France instead of Italy. Another time I saw an actor destroy a $1,000 prop because he "couldn't work with it!" Yet another time another actor refused to let anyone take a still picture of the set when he was on it unless he was paid $1,000 a photograph! I saw an actor scream at a musical director so severely that she broke down into tears in front of everyone (the string section offered to beat the crap out of him between shows). One time a celebrity showed up two-and-a-half days late on a three-day shoot and made the crew shoot the entire video in four hours. I've seen actors walk off sets and leave projects unfinished because they had tickets to a ball game. It is important to remember that the world does not revolve around you. It may seem to, but it doesn't. The kind of things I'm describing happen every day. If you get to the point in your career that you have weight, do everybody around you a favor and don't throw it around. If you throw it around, it will come back to haunt you. Be nice to the people around you. I've discovered that they are always doing their best to make my job easier; do the same in return.

Another thing to remember is to treat your agents with the respect with which you expect them to treat you with. As I mentioned earlier, a relationship with an agent is a symbiotic one. If you become a star, remember that you weren't always on top. Be loyal to the people who helped you when you needed it. There is an old expression that is very true: You meet the same people on the way down that you met on the way up. I never burn a bridge in my business relationships. It can't possibly hurt to be nice to people, but once you've made a memorable negative impression on someone, there is no going back. Just because you've outgrown a particular type of job it doesn't mean you will never need to go back to doing that type of job again some day. Once an actor plays a lead on a series, many times they will refuse to do anything but leads. Sometimes these people go years between jobs! Oftentimes their careers are ended by this kind of behavior, but they don't know it until it is too late. Actors falling out of choice movie roles refuse to take television parts. If you do this as a business, remember to keep your ego in check. Keep working and doing a good job at what you do. It is better to stay in the mix of working actors than to stay home and brood. Working keeps your career financially solvent. If you do an incredible job with the opportunities you get, people will notice and your career may get a boost. No one will notice you if you just stay home and wait for the phone to ring. Do the best you can with the opportunities you get. Don't become a pain in the butt to your agent by not wanting to take the kind of jobs they can get you. Keep your options open. But, above all, no matter what happens, be nice to the people around you. People will then think well of you.

CHAPTER TWENTY-TWO

I Could Have Been
a Retiree...
(Pension and Welfare)

What do you think of when you think of retirement? Miami Beach? Prunes? Clothes you wouldn't be caught dead in? Sunshine? Heat? The Old Actor's Home? These are things you might not dwell on when you're young. But they are things that you will find yourself thinking about some day. It takes an incredibly optimistic, goal-oriented individual to make a success of an acting career. Starting a career is more top-of-mind than completing a career. But even *Chorus Line* eventually closed. Personally, I could not imagine a time when I would not want to act. George Burns acted until he was 100. There is not much competition at that age, so if you live that long, it might be a time when your career really blossoms. You never know. Since this is a business book, I want you to think like an executive and consider things that you might not want to — but should.

When you are young, the sun always shines and nothing

ever hurts. As you get older, it rains and your bones ache. The older you get, the more it rains. You get the idea. Unless you are fabulously wealthy, you need to prepare for retirement and bad health. The earlier you prepare, the better off you will be. One of the hardest acting jobs I ever had was playing a prospective client for an insurance agent. It took a solid month to shoot the video. Another actor played an insurance agent who came to my home and sold me every type of insurance imaginable. If you've ever spent time with an aggressive insurance agent, you can imagine how long that month seemed. I had lines like: "Gee, I never thought of that" and "Sounds like a good idea to me. What about you, Honey?" I not only learned about every type of insurance, but why you should have it. Insurance is not hip. It is boring and sensible. It is for married people with kids and houses — not actors whose life is the theater! Well, one day you might find that there is more to life than the theater; you might learn that the theater is about life, and real life is a lot more unpredictable than a script. One day you might find yourself with a spouse and children, with a house and a yard. They will all count on you. Insurance is part of counting on you. You need to know about health insurance, dental insurance, life insurance, auto insurance, home insurance, liability insurance, and business-interruption insurance. Let's start with the easy ones.

HEALTH INSURANCE. Everybody has to have health insurance. You will need to have this even if you aren't an actor. All the actors' unions will provide you with health insurance. The first union you join will be your primary source of insurance; the second union will be your secondary, and so on. Each plan will provide you with certain benefits. You need to do a little research to find out exactly what you are covered for. Your primary union will cover most of the cost, and the other unions will pick up most of whatever is left over. Here is the biggest problem with union insurance coverage: You only get it when you have worked enough to qualify. Each calendar year, you must make minimum amounts to get benefits in each of the unions. You might make $30,000 a year, but you will not get any coverage because you have not made the required minimum in any of the unions. This can get to be a real problem. If your family is covered by these plans, they lose coverage, too. It takes ten years of making required minimums in each union to get fully vested. Once you are fully vested you won't have to worry, but until that time you'll have to stay on top of the situation. There will be times you will qualify for health insurance, and there will be times you won't. You'll have to cover yourself during the times you won't. If you are married, your spouse may have health insurance for the family. If you're not married, you will have to have a source to turn to. There is generally a waiting period before you are covered so don't wait until it is too late. The good news is that the union insurance policies are sufficient to cover you in most instances. If you are working in at least two of the unions, your health insurance needs will be taken care of. As I mentioned, each union's coverage is different so be familiar with what the union is providing. Since the union changes plans from time to time, it is a good idea to do a yearly review of your coverage for health and dental insurance.

LIFE INSURANCE. Most people avoid the subject of life insurance. If I'm dead, why do I need insurance? Life insurance is for your family. If you die, your life insurance is what they survive on. The unions don't give you much life insurance. It is cheap term insurance. AFTRA gives you $30,000, SAG gives you $10,000, but Equity gives you none. Forty thousand dollars might seem like a decent amount, but if you have a family, that might pay the bills for a year or two. You need to know about life insurance. Term insurance is good when you are starting out. When you are young and healthy, it costs very little to buy a lot of insurance because the odds of your dying are very slim. As you get older, it costs more each year because the odds of your dying increase with age. Term insurance has no loan value and you pay on it until the day you die. For actors, I recommend whole-life insurance. Whole-life insurance costs more than term insurance, but it has some significant advantages for the independent businessperson. Whole-life insurance builds value each year you pay for it. Your payments will never go up. If you pay for your policy enough years, the dividends earned by the policy will pay for themselves in subsequent years and even increase in value. When you reach retirement age, you have the option of cashing it in for cash. You can also take loans against a whole-life insurance policy. Banks like whole-life insurance policies because they have cash value. You can use a whole-life insurance policy as collateral. If you buy whole-life insurance when you are young, it will cost less to buy it than if you wait until you are older. Buy as much of it as you can early in your career. Since the payments will not increase over the years, the payments will not seem like much after the first five or six years since hopefully you will be making more money. Whole-life insurance can really stabilize an actor's financial life. Invest in it early if you can. Remember, only use SAG and AFTRA life insurance as a supplement to your other insurance plans.

AUTO INSURANCE. If you own a car, you must have insurance. But, when a car is a business expense, auto insurance is a deductible expense. My acting business owns a car. I use it to go to and from auditions and jobs. It is used for work. I have another car for personal use. IRS regulations change each year so check with your accountant if there is any tax advantage in owning a car for your business.

HOUSE INSURANCE and **LIABILITY INSURANCE.** These two types of insurance are linked together for a reason. If you keep a legitimate office in your home for your acting business, you may be able to write it off along with a portion of your homeowner's insurance costs. Make sure that you are using your office for your acting business. Be able to prove that you are using your office to make business calls, store promotional materials, organize mailings, and so on, so you can write-off the expenses. That's the good news. The bad news is that sometimes actors get sued. If you are in the public eye, a lot of attention is focused on you. You have to be careful of what you do and what you say. We live in a society that likes to sue public figures for things they say and do. You need to have liability insurance if that happens. When you are starting out, it is immaterial; but some day you might be making big bucks and then you should have it. When you are in the public eye, people look at you and wonder if you are vulnerable. If you are a TV star and touch somebody's car, they recognize you and see dollar signs. If you ever start making a lot of money, it pays to have good liability insurance.

BUSINESS-INTERRUPTION INSURANCE. If your career is rolling along, you will start to buy things. You will buy a house, a car, furniture, a boat, and so forth. Usually you will spend more than you have figuring your career can only go upward — but then something happens. You're a singer and you lose your voice; you're a dancer and you tear a knee ligament; you're a stage actor and you break your leg when you get hit by a jealous out-of-work actor driving a cab up and down Broadway. Suddenly your income ends and you find you have over-extended your resources. This is what business-interruption insurance is for. After you have a history of business activity, you can apply for it. If something happens, the insurance company will pay your bills for an extended period of time. Aren't you glad I did that insurance video? Insurance isn't fun, but if you're going to run a business, learn how insurance can help your acting career.

I'd also like to say a few words about retirement plans. All the unions have retirement plans. To qualify for a pension in any of them, you have to have earned a qualifying amount in ten different years for each union. You can get pensions from all the unions. The amount of money you receive each year will depend on how much money you earn in each union. The more you earn during your career, the larger your pension will be. In other words, you'll have a regular pension check just like if you worked for a big company. To supplement your pension, an actor can maintain other retirement plans like an IRA (Individual Retirement Account) or a Keogh Plan. Spending money on insurance and investing in retirement plans seem foolish when you're young, but it seems very wise when you get older. Every good business takes care of its employees; remember to take care of yourself.

CHAPTER TWENTY-THREE

I Could Have Been
a Fortune-Teller...
(New Business Opportunities)

Have you ever met a fortune-teller? A lot of them are pretty good actors. They can look you right in the eye and tell you whatever you want to know in such a way that you couldn't possibly believe that it wasn't absolutely true. They have an uncanny sense of drama. They can manipulate your emotions. Best of all, these people know everything that is going to happen in the future. The thing that puzzles me, though, is why are these people always poor? With their talent to predict the future, why aren't some of them on the board of directors of big companies that are struggling? If these people know what the future holds, why aren't they helping more big companies and holding down lucrative positions? "I'd like you to meet our board of directors. This is our CEO, this is our president, and this is our fortune-teller who will guide us into the next decade."

How many actors are good enough performers to apply

for the job of fortune-teller? I think I could be a good one. It would not be difficult for a casting director to imagine me in a gypsy wagon gazing into a crystal ball while the smell of incense helped me work my magic. (After all, I lived through the sixties.) I don't think I'd use a crystal ball to predict the future, though. I think I'd opt to use statistics. Recently, I wrote a video for Valparaiso University. The university had been trying to raise the money to build a performing arts center for the past three decades. They had made very little progress. I analyzed the situation and took an approach that I thought would appeal to corporate donors. The video was called *Windows of Opportunity.* The new performing arts center was going to have a lot of windows in it, but those kind of windows are unimportant to corporate donors. The windows that were important to them were video screens. In the video, I predicted that the largest growing job market in the near future would be THE PERFORMING ARTS! Actors, writers, musicians, and graphics artists would experience a volume of growth in job opportunities greater than at any other time in history.

In less than a few months, the money was raised for the new performing arts center. Why did a three-decade exercise in futility turn around so quickly? I knew what I was talking about, and anybody and everybody at the top of the business world knew it. The new performing arts center is now brick and mortar, and I was the first Valparaiso University speech and drama major ever to win the Alumni Achievement Award at the "Harvard of the Midwest." What does this mean to you? There is going to be more acting work than ever in the very near future. Earning a living as an actor is going to be possible for more people than ever before. The number of video screens in the world are increasing at an astonishing rate. The amount of time people spend in front of video screens is also increasing at an astonishing rate. Who is going to fill those screens? Actors. Lots and lots of actors. In the last ten years, the number of stations on television has grown twenty-fold. In the next ten years, the increase will be even more dramatic. Cable has 1,000 potential windows right now, and the Internet has an infinite number available. Programming, interactive television, niche movies, talking books, network gaming, and entertainment options that haven't been invented yet will need to be created for all these "windows." At first, cable survived on old reruns; now more new programming than ever before is being created — and that is good news for actors. Other windows are creating new opportunities for actors. How many actors do you see or hear on your computer? Actors appear in games and educational computer applications. Animation is creating narration and other voice-over jobs. Technology has gotten simpler and more affordable. Digital has changed the world. *Wayne's World* started off as a joke; now it is affordable reality. I saw an ad for local-access cable networks; the asking price was $1,000 for an entire network. Buy a couple of digital video cameras and a video-editing program for your computer and you're a network tycoon. Young filmmakers are making niche videos and creating stars overnight. *The Blair Witch Project* is a great example. It first appeared on the Internet as a hoax. People who found it thought it was for real. They thought it was an event instead of a film. Home video quality lowered production costs and made it more believable. It is possible to make good movies for a few hundred thousand dollars — or less. A student film I worked on was done for $1,000 and a lot of effort and begging. It won an Academy Award for Best Student Film of the Year in 1972. It was a tribute to Alfred Hitchcock; Hitchcock actually watched the film and called the director to say how much he enjoyed it. In the past, if you wanted to be in the movies, you had to get involved with the big guys in Hollywood. Now, there is room for the little guy to make movies, too. It's too bad Ed Wood isn't alive and making movies today; the Internet and cable were made for his kind of filmmaking.

A world of remarkable opportunity is emerging for our industry. Because of digital technology and fiber-optic telephone lines, studios all over the world can be linked. Currently, live audio sessions are conducted over these lines. Using this technology, a director in Chicago can direct talent in New York but record them in Chicago; for all practical purposes, it is just like the talent is in the studio in Chicago. Currently, video files can be transmitted over these lines and then downloaded. This means an editor in one city can show his work to a director in another city without waiting for tapes to be shuttled back and forth. The process takes minutes instead of days. The end result is the speed of these transmissions is starting to decentralize the industry. Soon, you'll be able to live anywhere you want and still be involved in the business. Many well-known announcers now work out of their homes in small studios over digital phone lines. The expression "phoning it in" is now a reality. Fiber-optic cables are being installed everywhere so that digital information technology will be accessible in every business and home. Everything will come through these lines. You'll be able to see any movie ever made on your home video screen instantaneously by simply dialing in a code. Network television, cable television, Internet programming, and other types of programming we haven't even imagined yet will also come through these digital lines. I'm sure that even books will be video-ized and come into your home through "windows." For example, you'll probably be able to pick up your telephone and dial in an Emeril Lagasse recipe that will be delivered to your kitchen monitor by a video version of Emeril. Why read a recipe when Emeril can appear on a video screen in your kitchen and show you how to do it step-by-step himself? His presence will be interactive so you can work at your own pace. Windows of opportunity will open for actors with each technological advance. We are just at the beginning.

So when your parents question your choice of occupation and choice of college curriculum, point out the very salient facts I've just presented. The arts will be entering an era of prosperity. You will still have the echelons of stakes, handicap, and allowance actors, but the number of claiming actors that earn livable incomes will significantly increase. They will face the same business problems I have described in this book, but their chances of success will be better. Big business reacted favorably to my video because it presented a realistic prediction of the future based upon statistics and empirical data. It is how business works. People can smell a phony a mile away (the fortune-teller's incense is a dead giveaway). Don't kid yourself about your future. If you want to be a success, do the homework it takes to plan out a successful future. I could have been a fortune-teller. . . I could have, I could have!

CHAPTER TWENTY-FOUR

I Could Have Been a Lecturer...
(Quality Control)

This book is based upon the lectures I have given at universities over the past twenty-five years. I started giving the lectures to provide students with information I couldn't obtain while I was in school. I wanted to make sure students got a better education in the business of acting than I did. So, over the years, I asked students what questions they had and what worried them, and then I did my best to find answers to their questions. In many cases, I discovered that students were so overwhelmed by the task of figuring out how to get into the acting business, they did not even know which questions to ask. Hopefully, I have anticipated and answered those questions, too. One thing I do know is that over the years students have always been grateful that someone was willing to take the time to answer these questions. Professors have described my book as a "one-on-one talk with the actor." I think that's good because I was trying to capture my honest answers to honest questions asked by actors starting their careers. After my experience with the head of the Northwestern theater department, I set out on a mission to fill a void in every actor's education.

The kind of information I've talked about in this book is not the kind of knowledge a university professor can give you. They know about acting; I know about how to make money acting. I gained my knowledge by being a working actor who had a lot of successes and failures over a thirty-year period. It is street knowledge that will be vital to your survival. I related personal experiences and explained the importance of the lessons they taught me. When you win auditions, you gain money; when you lose auditions, you gain knowledge. Both are important if you intend to survive. I described stark reality and its relationship to heartfelt emotion. After reading this book, I think you'll have an idea of what it feels like to be me — not a star but a working professional actor. You'll know what kind of problems to anticipate, and some of the things you can do to solve them. You may not grasp everything I discuss completely upon your first reading. Some chapters will not make sense until you are many years into your career. But, hopefully this book will help move your career forward. For me it has been very gratifying to learn how many students have used my advice to help them begin and sustain their careers. A great many of them have stayed in touch, and I am proud to say many are making full-time livings as professionals in the business.

I wanted to make sure this book was going to be useful to aspiring actors and teachers, so I asked many actors and teachers to read it and give me reactions to it. I've made many adjustments based upon their suggestions. As I neared my final draft, a very serious concern was brought up. A professor asked me: "Was I making the business of acting sound too hard? Would students be discouraged?" These questions worried me. I certainly didn't want to discourage anyone from doing something they loved, but I wanted actors to make a career choice knowing the facts. The sad fact is acting is one of the most difficult career choices you can make. It isn't easy for anyone. It pits the best against the best — this means many more will fail than succeed, but the joyous fact is many of us do survive and prosper. I'm really glad I took the chance to defy the odds. If I had not taken that chance, I would never have had a chance to succeed. You will never know if you can become a professional actor until you try. Do you really want to live your life knowing you might have been an actor but didn't because you never gave it a try? Life is filled with wannabe actors who never tried and then said they could have done it. I'm glad I became a professional actor because the rewards were well worth the struggle.

It takes a tremendous effort have an acting career. When you start out it feels like you are standing at the foot of Mt. Everest with an impossible climb ahead of you. How could anyone get to the top? Well, it is possible, but you have to realize it is like any other difficult task — it takes a very long time, incredible persistence, and enough knowledge and talent to create game plans that work. There is no such thing as an overnight success in acting. Overnight successes make great stories for movies, but we all know movies that take two hours to watch don't take two hours to make. If you want a career, it will take work. No one can make it happen except you. To attempt to earn a living as an actor is an incredible challenge. So, I am not worried that anyone who really wants to earn a living as an actor will be discouraged by this book. Why? Because I know thoroughbreds love a challenge. A thoroughbred will win against all odds over all adversity no matter how serious the competition because it is in their blood. If someone really wants to act for a living, the information in this book will spur them forward — they will take the bit and run with it.

An actor friend called me recently. I had not spoken to him

in about five years. He was no longer earning his living as an actor. I mentioned this book to him, and we talked about it for a while. Since he knew me very well, he pointed something out about me to me that I think is worth passing on to you. He said he was always impressed with my "toughness." No matter how bad things got, I never let it get to me. I never quit or walked away from a problem. I never seemed to get discouraged or emotional when I failed. Failure always stiffened my resolve to win the next time. I don't get called tough a lot, but he was right: You have to be tough to make it as an actor. Like a thoroughbred, I have tunnel vision when it comes to winning. I block out emotion, pain, and losing when I'm competing for a job; I only focus on what I have to do to win. I don't get discouraged because I know I'm tough enough to push myself hard enough to win. So, don't be discouraged by the challenges this book lays out for you. Instead, look inside yourself and discover how badly you want to be an actor.

Over the years, it has been interesting to note how students' reasons for choosing an acting career have changed. The times greatly affect what people want out of an acting career, and the current cost of an education has greatly impacted the type of students interested in acting. The part of my lectures I have always enjoyed the most has been the question and answer segments with the students. It always gives me a pretty good idea of what is happening in their lives. When I was in college, Vietnam and protests were in. Theater and film students were rebels who were interested in acting because they wanted to express their anger and frustration in more theatrical protests. Acting was political. Art was everything, and entertainment sucked. Years later, Ronald Reagan was in office and the country was financially well-off; going to a university became very expensive. One acting student actually asked me how many months he would have to act before he could afford a BMW. At that time, acting was about making money in a hurry. More recently, because of the cost of an education, many students who would like to major in acting are hesitant because they think the risk factor is too great. But hopefully, the last chapter about new job opportunities created by digital technology will lift your spirits and give you renewed hope.

Speaking of renewed hope, something recently happened at Northwestern University during career night that I have thought about frequently ever since. There was a very serious-looking student sitting in the front row of the 250-seat lecture hall. She was furiously scribbling notes about everything I said. She had a huge stack of books with her and looked like the proverbial bookworm. When I opened the floor to questions, she immediately raised her hand and asked: " If I major in theater, will I be able to change the world?" The other students groaned or stifled laughs. As I looked at her, I could tell she was dead serious. What could I say to her? That is a big question. I had not asked myself that question in many years, but I am glad she asked it, because it took me back to the days when I was a student. I think every actor thinks about the answer to that question at some point in his or her life. But most often, it is when they are in the shower preparing their Academy Award acceptance speech. (If you are like most actors, you regularly give Academy Award acceptance speeches to your imaginary friends while you shower.) The difference here was that she had the courage to ask this question out loud. Hearing it out loud in front of a large group of people seemed silly. How big an ego do you have to have to think you are important enough to even think a thought like that? But if you want to act for a living, it has to hold that much importance for you. For you to be able to succeed as an actor, acting must be your life. You won't have time to drive a cab. You're going to be far too busy creating work that millions of people will see, so maybe you will get the chance to change the world.

When I began my acting career, people warned me that my chances of success were small, and yet I have managed to stay employed as a professional actor for over three decades. It is true that I am not a star. I am not a stakes horse, a handicap horse, or even an allowance horse. I am a very high level claiming horse, and occasionally, I get to run with the big boys; but I am still not one of them. I still have very high hopes that some day I will be one of them, but right now I'm not. George Burns didn't make it until he was nearly ninety years old, so I've still got decades of chances left. Some people might think I'm not qualified to write this book because I never became a star. But that alone is the single most important factor I possess that qualifites me to write this book. I know the business of acting as one of the guys. I found a way to survive in a very treacherous business. I made a living without a star's income. I found lots of jobs that paid small amounts of money instead of just a few huge jobs that paid a lot of money. A star might offer you a very different perspective of the business of acting, but that kind of information is very specific to one individual and is more appropriate for an inspirational autobiography about someone who made it to the top than a how-to guide for the beginner. What I have put forth in this book will hopefully give you a pretty good idea what you can do to keep yourself working at your craft. I didn't write a chapter on how to be a star because there are not enough jobs for everyone to be a star. If it happens to you, great; but don't bank on it. Just being a working actor for an entire career is a tremendous accomplishment. Be proud if it works out that way for you. Stardom is frosting on the cake. It can't happen for everyone.

If you are a thoroughbred, you'll know it. When you audition, the desire to succeed will ignite in you — and that desire will burn so bright nothing will stop you from attaining your goal. You will find yourself thinking of nothing else day and night. You'll always be looking for a new angle to make a go of it. I knew that I wanted to be a professional actor the last day I performed with the Repertory Company in Valparaiso, Indiana. After my last performance at the theater, I went back on the stage after the audience had left. The work light was on. I stood there and looked at the empty seats. The time I spent on that stage was the most fun I had ever had in my entire life. Audiences laughed and applauded me. I was paid a salary for my efforts. What an incredible way to make a living! The feeling of accomplishment was inspiring; the money was secondary. The thought that I might never have a chance to equal that feeling gave me a sense of emptiness and loss I could not bear. I knew that I had to find a way to keep doing what I loved to do. Every time I perform, I feel the same way. It means that much to me. When you're around incredibly good actors, you will sense the same thing about them. They only know how to give a maximum effort 100 percent of the time. They are true thoroughbreds in every sense of the word. Their craft is vitally important to them. It is at the center of their being.

Acting is not something you do as a lark. It requires intensity to compete. Competition among actors for work is fierce because the rewards for performing are great. People pay attention to you. People admire you. People respect you. People think you're cool and want to be like you. Actors are loved. People applaud your accomplishments. They want to know about you. They pat you on the back and make you feel swell. All you have to do is be you. Some people will like you so much that they just might give you millions and millions of dollars some day. So is it any wonder that so many people want to be actors? It is an ultimate job.

Whether or not you make it will depend upon you. Only you know if you want it badly enough. No one can give you an acting career. No one can buy you an acting career. The odds are stacked greatly against you. If you are not completely committed, the odds are even longer. But anything of worth is always difficult to attain. Being committed enough to want to change the world is a good place to start. When I started, I wanted to change the world; I wanted to end the war and teach people to love each other. That's probably why I became an actor. People spend a lot of time watching and listening to actors. Make the time they spend watching and listening to you worth their time.

I have not achieved what I set out to do. Hardly anyone ever accomplishes all their goals. But I set my sights very high to keep me motivated. I still wake up each morning with my sights set on becoming a successful actor who will play a role that people will remember. In addition to my acting, I write plays and movies about things that mean something to me that I think are worth passing along. Every once in a while, I get to play a character that I think is important for an audience to see. Those are the things that keep me going. Every actor needs to find something important enough to motivate them past the bad times. Artists are interested in ideas. To succeed as an actor, it helps to believe in something enough that it will drive you forward toward your end goal. It has to be more than money because eventually, you can get enough of that. You have to go deep inside yourself to find out what it is. Only you can discover the answer to this question.

I had the talent and education to become many different things in life — an accountant, a banker, a soldier, a teacher, an executive, an ad man, a blue-collar worker, or the owner of a cab company. But, I didn't become any of those things. The desire to enter any of those other occupations was never there. I would have only done those jobs to make a buck. In some cases, I probably could have made a lot more money, but I would not have been happy. In the end, I became an actor because in my heart it was the only thing I could become. If you find that same feeling in you, perhaps acting is the profession for you!

PART TWO

BUSINESS AND ART

Many actors find it difficult to mix business and art. They think financial considerations taint art. Professional actors make art their business. They know that it takes money to make art. The professional actor's art is so good and so much in demand that audiences will pay to see it. But the art of actors at the highest levels is not created in a vacuum; professional actors learn to work with artists of many other disciplines — writers, directors, producers, musicians, scenic artists, makeup artists, journalists, publicists, and many others. How well actors relate to others greatly affects their business. This section contains practical suggestions to help the actor sustain a career while achieving a balance between art and business.

CHAPTER TWENTY-FIVE

I Could Have Been a Method Actor...
(Troubleshooting)

Y ou learn to talk the talk. You learn to walk the walk. If you want to hang around the block, that is what you need to do. Growing up in Cicero, Illinois, the home of Al Capone, that is what you want to do. You learn to blend into your environment so you don't get beat up. Actors spend a lot of time learning to blend in. That is the essence of art. When I went to college in Valparaiso, Indiana, I did not instantly blend in. In 1966, very few college students wore Banlon shirts, shark-skin pants, and alligator shoes. I'm glad I had the good sense to pack one pair of white jeans, a couple of madras shirts, and a pair of penny loafers.

When I first started studying acting in college, I had never taken an acting class before. So I was a blank page. When I was in class, I listened a lot and didn't talk much; blank pages blend in better that way. As the actors chattered away about their roles, our acting coach, Dr. Fred Sitton, would say:

"Don't talk about it. Do it." That made the other actors mad; they wanted to study Method acting, they wanted to study Stanislavski, they wanted to study Grotowski. I put all this in the back of my mind during the next three years of acting classes. I bought some books and did some reading on my own. Since I was going to be attending Northwestern University for graduate school, I figured I better have some knowledge about the different schools of acting. Even though I wasn't formally trained in Method or Stanislavski, I figured I could fake it. But I was worried. In reality, I knew more about Kabuki than I did about Method. However, since I worked as a professional actor for three years before going to graduate school, no one ever questioned my methods. Much to my surprise, I never got to take a Method class in graduate school because Northwestern didn't offer it. If your heart is beating faster with indignation, read on: This chapter was written for you.

When Dustin Hoffman was shooting *Marathon Man* with Laurence Olivier, he wanted to look haggard for a scene. He deprived himself of sleep and showed up on set looking awful. He told Olivier what he had done and Olivier replied: "Try acting, dear boy." Ingrid Bergman once asked Alfred Hitchcock why she should do something in a scene (i.e., what was her motivation); Hitchcock replied: "Because I told you to." When you get out into the real world, don't try to impress people with what you know about acting. The lighting technician won't bore you with endless talk about key lights and Hubble twist locks to impress you with what he or she knows about lighting. The makeup person won't try to impress you with unnecessary information about the difference between Stein pancake and Mabeline pancake. You might think you're more important than these people, but you're not. They are replaceable and so are you. The point I'm trying to make here is that people are more interested in the end result of what you do than in how you go about doing it. Actors who have been trained in very stringent technique schools frequently have tunnel vision. They learn to approach acting from only one viewpoint and find it difficult if everyone doesn't solve problems the way that they do. They need a lot of time to work through their process of characterization. Unfortunately, the business doesn't work that way. Time is money, and these actors must learn to adjust quickly or else they find themselves out of the business.

Technique is an individual thing. Whatever works for you is great. If you plan on getting into television or the movies, you need to develop a technique that produces results quickly. In acting school, you work through scenes very slowly and in great detail. While you are in school, you are learning to do something, so you want to take your time. When you get out into the real world, people will expect you to be proficient and efficient at building characters. Many actors come to the business anticipating that they will have long periods of time to work on a character. They expect to have long meetings and discussions with the director and other actors. In the vast majority of cases, this will not happen. Ensemble theater companies that are funded will occasionally operate in this manner. These types of companies are usually nonprofit organizations who are associated with schools. Professional (for profit) theater companies, motion picture companies, and television production companies all operate on very stringent timetables and budgets. Commercials happen even quicker. They don't have time for you to go through a process to get into character. They expect you to show up ready to perform the character you were hired to do. If you need to go through a long involved process to create your character, do it on your own time, by yourself, at home; don't try doing it on the set. If the director doesn't like what you've created, be able to abandon what you've prepared and respond to what the director tells you to do instantaneously. "Just do it!" Why? "Because the director told you to." Remember: "Try acting."

I've had the opportunity to work on television shows and movies with some pretty famous directors. Television has really stringent schedules. If a director can't get the job done on time and budget, the studios will not tolerate it. I was doing a one-hour drama show, and the director fell two hours behind on the second day of the shoot (Tuesday). By ten o'clock that night the decision was made to fire him. Another director was hired that night and flown into Chicago by six o'clock the next morning. When I saw him on the set, I said I was surprised to see him; he said he was surprised to be there, too, because he was just sitting around the house the previous night with no plans for the next day. He had just barely read the script when he stepped on the set. He expected all the actors to know what they were doing in each scene. His main priority was to get things moving to get the show back on schedule. Another time I was working on a one-hour drama with the L.A.'s hottest director that year. He had just won the Emmy for best director. I was really looking forward to working with him. I was doing a scene with an actress, Lucy Childs, and she was excited about working with this director, too. When you do a one-scene part on a television series or a movie, you rarely see the entire script; in most cases, you just receive sides of the scenes you're in. I read my sides and confided to Lucy that I really didn't understand the scene. She confided to me that she didn't get it either. We talked about the scene and ran lines and assumed the director would tell us what he wanted when he got there. Well, when he got there, he said: "You know, I read this scene and I don't have any idea what's going on here. Let's just shoot it and see what happens." Not all directors work like this, but many do. Don't be surprised or disappointed if you find yourself in this kind of situation. It's just the nature of the business. When you act in television shows or movies, it's not like performing Shakespeare where each word is precious and you don't deviate from the script. "Whatever works" is how many movies are done. There is a big difference between original scripts and classics everyone knows. Original scripts are works in progress; they are living, breathing organisms that are being created and shaped by the people working on them. Scenes come and go. Things are rewritten on the set. The truest words ever spoken to me were said by Mickey Rooney. I was writing a project for him, and I was really working hard to make the script perfect. Here are his words of advice: "Just write it and don't worry about it because when we do it, we're going to do what we do anyway." When you're acting professionally, be prepared to be flexible. Be prepared to "do it" — now. Be prepared to trust your instincts and just let it fly.

I think it is valuable for every actor to study Stanislavski. It teaches you all the basics (i.e., Who am I? What do I want? Why does my character do this? etc.). But, everyone has not studied Stanislavski. In fact, many actors have not studied at all. They just "do it," and many of them do it very successfully. If you don't believe me, wait until you do your first scene with a kid or a dog. A kid or a dog can steal any scene with genuine naïveté. Acting can be that simple. Sometimes it's just natural. I have personally found it valuable to study many different acting techniques and to be knowledgeable about each of them. I think it is very important to have control over your craft. It is wonderful to be able to just let it happen naturally, but that doesn't always work. A lot of actors are "it" for awhile, but their careers fail once they have fallen out of style. They can't be anything but what they naturally are. Learning acting technique gives you more control. But I am not a purist who clings to one technique and cannot acknowledge the existence of any other.

Being able to approach an acting problem from many different angles has solved many problems for me. Personally, I found improv classes to be the most valuable. When you are a professional, speed is of the essence. Improv teaches you to think on your feet and improve your mental dexterity. Auditions happen like train wrecks — they happen fast and if you want to win, you need to make a big impact. If what you've prepared is all wrong, you'll need to create a new approach immediately. Improv teaches that skill. Many times my studies in dance, mime, and Kabuki have solved acting problems with physical solutions instead of intellectual ones. I've learned to stand outside my character and watch him move to see if there is anything I can enhance strictly through the use of movement. Dancers, mimes, and Kabuki actors create very individual characters and tell entire stories using only movement. And of course, modeling has taught me to communicate complicated messages with a single picture. These are things you don't necessarily consider in Stanislavski, but they come in very handy on a movie set when you're making pictures.

When an audience watches an actor, they respond to what they see and hear. The work an actor puts into preparing for the role is for the actor not the audience. It always boils down to one thing: What did you "do." If what you "do" does not produce the desired effect for an audience or a director, it is wrong. Many times an actor will try to justify what he has "done" by explaining the process he went through to create the action. All the reasons might be completely logical and justifiable, but it doesn't matter if the audience can't see or hear it. Audiences do not see an actor's motivations; that happens inside the actor's mind. There is nothing more boring than watching someone think. Many actors who are purists to Stanislavki or Method techniques have trouble adjusting their thinking on set. I know I did at first. Sometimes, you just need to trust your director and do what you are told to do even though it doesn't make sense to your acting technique. I know that Ingrid Bergman learned to trust Alfred Hitchcock, and the results certainly bore out that trust. I have learned to use other acting techniques like improv, dance, mime, and Kabuki to make quick adjustments to my characters. They don't always answer the basic Stanislavski questions, but they work. When you are a professional, it is important to have a bag of acting tricks at your disposal to solve problems quickly. Audiences respond to what they see and hear — not to your acting approach or technique. No one really cares how you created your character, so develop an acting technique that works for you.

I Could Have Been a Director...
(Delegation of Authority)

The actor/director relationship is a very special one. There is a lot of give-and-take involved. There is a lot of mutual respect. However, there are as many different schools of directing as there are schools of acting — especially in television and film. If you plan on having a career, you'll need to learn to develop good working relationships with a wide variety of directors. In theater, you'll generally find directors with university theater backgrounds who have studied a lot of acting. If you are right out of a university theater department, you will feel very comfortable with these directors. However in film, television, and commercials, directors come from many varied disciplines — they are graphic artists, photographers, writers, rock musicians, actors, IASTE teamsters, and so on. In fact, many directors work their way up through the ranks from production assistants and have no formal training in film school. Film directors come from just about any walk of life. As a result, directors' techniques vary greatly. Different directors use different means to get the actor to "do" what they want. You will enjoy some of these methods and you will hate others. In any case, the actor has to be ready for anything.

One of my favorite directors is Bo May. We have worked together many times. When you work with someone a lot, you eventually develop a rapport that is second nature. While we were shooting a film, Bo walked up to me after a take and said: "Do it again, but this time give it a little more magenta." I knew just what he meant. Another time, I was directed to "JoBeize" it; in other words, I was supposed to be more like myself and less like what I was trying to be. You just never know how you are going to be directed. Personally, I like directors who use a lot of creativity in their direction. It can make for a challenging, fun day when you are asked to act in magenta. But some directors offer no latitude when they give a direction. They are not interested in getting an actor's input. They will show you what to do and exactly how to do it or say it. It is especially difficult when you mimic them exactly and they are displeased with the results. Then they do the same thing again, and you copy it exactly again, and they are displeased again. That can make for a very long day. Be patient and keep an open mind.

Directing art can be difficult because turning ideas into realities needs a lot of translations along the way. Fifty different directors would turn out fifty different pieces of art from the same script. One of the most insightful explanations of the creative process of art that I have ever heard came from Rick Steinman, the writer of many of the Raid Bug Killer commercials. His client asked Rick why his commercials never looked the way he thought they would look. Rick explained it to me this way. He asked the man to imagine ten executives sitting around a table together. They all wanted to have lunch. He gives each of them paper and pencil. Each executive must write down what his vision of lunch is. No one is allowed to look at what anyone else writes down. No one is allowed to eat lunch until every person's vision of lunch is exactly the same. Needless to say, all the executives starve to death and Rick gets to go off and do the commercial his way. Not even an infinite amount of verbiage will adequately describe to someone what you see in your mind's eye.

A director has a vision. There are no words that will allow him to perfectly describe what he is after. In the professional world, most directors keep going until they get exactly what they want. They may give you many different directions as they hone in on what they want you to "do." When Bo told me to use more magenta, I knew he didn't like the last take and wanted me to try something a little bolder. He didn't want me to go completely nuts or else he would have told me to use red. I kept varying my approach until I made him happy.

I have worked as an actor and as a director. My personal belief is that the director is in charge of the project. I do my best to achieve his or her vision because he or she is the only artist with a complete overall view of the entire project. If I don't agree with the vision, I still do my best to make to make it happen. Many times our visions are exactly the same, but we are using different words to describe them. I believe the actor is a part of the project rather than the whole project. The actor views a project from the actor's needs and wants. The director views the project from the production's needs and wants. Because the director is always privy to information that the actor does not have, I defer to the director's judgment. As a businessman, I have always tried to make the director's job as easy as possible. That doesn't mean I don't ask questions and make suggestions; it means that I am more interested in help-ing the director achieve his or her goals than in fulfilling my personal agenda. I trust the directors I work with; the power to make me look good is in their hands.

Personally, I think a director has a better perspective of the project than anyone else because the director is the viewing audience. The actor does not stand outside the scene and observe; that is the director's job. Not only does the director hold the artistic vision of the project, but he or she knows the business problems of the project as well. The director knows what needs to be done and what the production budget will allow to be done. Compromises caused by budget are a great challenge to every director. The actor only has knowledge of what he or she wants to do. The director has a much broader perspective. Remember you are doing a job because the director asked you to be there. Don't bite the hand that feeds you and your family. Directors frequently use the same actors over and over again, so do your best to develop a good relationship with directors who use you. There are a whole lot more actors than directors, so treat the directors who hire you well.

CHAPTER TWENTY-SEVEN

I Could Have Been a Jack-of-All-Trades...

(Do-It-Yourselfers in the Workplace)

If you are getting the impression that I know a lot about many different things and that I am very competent at each of them, then you are getting the idea behind this book. Earning a living as an artist is a very difficult proposition. But you'll notice that many successful artists have the ability to do it all. Clint Eastwood started as an actor, but he became a very successful director and producer. He has used his other talents to keep his acting career going. Woody Allen started as a writer and stand-up comedian and became an actor and director. Harold Pinter went from playwriting to acting. Mike Nichols and Elaine May are two of The Second City's most famous alumni. Each of them eventually surpassed their acting careers with writing, directing, and producing careers. Most actors have interests in other arts — writing, directing, producing, photography, music, dance, opera, and so forth. You'll find that there are a lot of interconnections between most of these disciplines. Most successful actors spend spare time developing their interests in these skills and frequently use them to advance their acting careers. Of course for the skills to become an asset to one's business, they must be developed to a professional level. But then again, William Shatner's vocal albums are collectors' items! Because they were so bad in a campy way, they launched a new phase of his career. Time and greater successes have allowed him to distance himself from them and laugh at them like everyone else.

Once I started working as an actor and spending a lot of time on sets and in studios, I realized I had a lot of time with nothing to do. Acting is like the army in that "you hurry up and wait." Unless you're playing a lead, you spend a lot of time waiting. You can spend endless hours reading paperbacks and drinking coffee, or you can get more involved. When I was in college, I did not study film; I studied acting and writing. So when I started working on films, I wanted to learn as much as I could as quickly as I could so I could fit in. I made it a point to get to know everyone on the set and understand what each person did. I'd talk to the script person and try to figure out how notes were kept and how close to copy the script had to be. I'd ask the lighting crew about how different effects were achieved. I learned about key lights and fill lights and how to "feel" the light. I talked with camera operators so I could understand my framing and learned how to vary my movements to make the camera crew's job simpler. I'd talk to the sound crew about the things I could do to keep my body microphone from rubbing on my clothes and ruining the sound in shots. After I built my recording studios, I was able to build a very fine business doing sound finishing of motion pictures and commercials with the knowledge I gained on location. This gave me an advantage over most studio owners who have never been on location. I used my idle time on sets to improve my producer skills, too. As things went wrong, I made notes of why and what could be done in the future to make the process of filmmaking more efficient. My production company recently completed its 5,500th consecutive project without going over budget on a single project. Needless to say, I learned a lot by other people's mistakes. As a result, I own a very profitable production company that means I will always have a future in the business. Like many other successful actors, I have found a way to create employment for myself.

When I was in the Bridge-VU Repertory Company, it was a very formative time for me. I learned quickly that no actor always gets lead parts. I did twenty-six plays with the company, but I only played a lead every third or fourth show. When I played smaller roles or chorus parts in musicals, I found myself with time on my hands so I learned to build and paint scenery, design and run lights, and operate sound. I even learned to do props and makeup. While I did these things, I made extra money and learned how other actors related to these other theater crafts. I observed firsthand how actors who liked to change their blocking made life very difficult for the lighting crew. I later sat in meetings and heard technical people tell directors that some actors were problems and saw how that influenced who got which roles. Becoming a jack-of-all-theater-trades taught me to look at actors from many different points of view. That in turn taught me to look at myself in a whole new way.

People frequently refer to me as a Renaissance Man. They are amazed at all the different things I can do. I, on the other hand, am always amazed at all the things I can't do yet. Remember what I told you earlier: Acting is doing. Producers hire people who can do. Each skill I picked up along the way has won acting roles for me. I bring a lot to a role when I am playing an accountant, a horse handicapper, a hockey player, a business executive, a soldier, a golf pro, a lighting technician, a Renaissance Man, or any of the other occupations I could have become because I have done each of these things. I have a wide range of experiences and skills to draw on. I'm always learning to do somethng new. Most recently, I've been learning to drive race cars. Why am I constantly pushing myself to learn to do new things? It's a new challenge and increases my potential to play new kinds of roles. I've been hired to drive large earth-moving equipment and trucks in previous film projects because of my extensive experience in the army with tanks and other forms of motorized vehicles. Who would have thought that this skill would be valuable to an actor? Tanks got me acting work! James Garner got the part in *Grand Prix* because he could actually drive the race cars. I've always found his work in that movie one of the great acting accomplishments of all time. Unless you've driven a race car, it is hard to comprehend his achievement. It is not something everyone can do. The thing that impressed me most about *Mission Impossible II* was that Tom Cruise did his own rock climbing in the movie. It was something he wanted to do for himself. If you want people to watch you act, make sure you can do something special so that you don't disappoint them.

After my work as the silent spokesman for Cheer detergent won the Golden Lion award at the Cannes Film Festival, Proctor & Gamble decided to try redoing the commercial for other products in other countries. They figured they could show my commercials to actors in those countries and they could "do" what I did. They tested a German "JoBe" in Germany and an Italian "JoBe" in Italy. In both cases, the campaign failed. The actors looked like me, but they could not "do" what I did. There was a nuance to my performance that made it one of a kind (thank goodness!). As a result, I extended my success with Cheer into sixteen other countries for Proctor & Gamble. I even won best commercial of the year in

Venezuela. What created the nuance in my performance that made it hard to duplicate? My experiences "doing" things. When I was in college, I spent a lot of time studying comedy movement. I studied silent film acting (Chaplin was just a small part of my studies). I studied Comedia Del'Arte and focused on Lazi (an Italian word referring to silent comedy bits) used by Comedia troupes. When I was in musicals and got stuck in a chorus part, I'd always talk the director into letting me do Lazi in the big dance numbers to add more comedy to the show. Once I became known for this, I elevated many a chorus part into a good part for me. I wouldn't have a line in the show, and yet I managed to get big laughs and make the audience want to see more of me. When I was at The Second City, I frequently did scenes in which I played silent characters. I spent nearly twenty years on a stage learning how to make an audience laugh using physical humor. All the things that I learned to "do" came together in the Cheer commercial. My skill was very difficult to duplicate because I developed it in a very unique way. At the time I studied Lazi and silent film, I didn't foresee that a role would come along that was custom-made for my physical style of humor. That is why I encourage you to learn to do as many different things as possible. You'll never know when your skills as a jack-of-all-trades will come in handy and make you special for an acting role.

Most people advise actors to have a "survival job," and by this they mean a job driving a cab or waiting tables to keep money flowing in while you find acting work. My advice is that "career survival" is a more worthwhile goal. Spend your time "doing" things that will keep you close to acting. If you have a job working lights or building scenery, you'll gain a different perspective on actors like I did. If you are a writer, producer, or director, you'll gain a different perspective on actors. If you're playing in the band for a musical, you'll gain yet another perspective. While these jobs aren't acting jobs, you still get to study acting and learn to relate to it in a totally different way. Sometimes you learn that these artistic skills can be more fully developed than your acting skills, but you won't know until you do them. In my career, my involvement in each new skill brought something unexpected to my acting. It didn't take me away from acting but rather helped me to understand it better.

I don't have to build or paint scenery to make money for survival; when I do it, I do it because I want to be hands-on with one of my ideas. I love to write and when I do it, I create jobs for myself. I learned to produce and direct as a necessary evil when I couldn't afford to hire someone to do it for me, but now I've gained a new respect for those jobs and look forward to doing them (and when I do, I frequently create acting work for myself). I never set out to own studios, but now I do, and I realize it made me more valuable as an actor. Being a Renaissance Man is nice — because it gives you choices. The more you can do, the more choices you get. Attaining a status where you can pick and choose your acting jobs is a position each actor should aspire to. Learn to do everything you can. When it comes to acting, a jack-of-all-trades, is a master of his or her career.

CHAPTER TWENTY-EIGHT

I Could Have Been a Clone...

(Individuality in the Workplace)

D id you ever have a dream in which everyone looked exactly like you? As you already know, I'm not a psychiatrist, so I can't tell you what a dream like that would mean. But, I am a professional actor, and I can tell you that you will have that experience many times during your career. Wait until you experience your first cattle call. Moo! Moo! Moo! I auditioned at Twentieth Century Fox for a Neil Simon pilot one year. I was exactly what the casting director was looking for; in fact, I was the 147th actor she had looked at that was perfect for the part. All the actors that auditioned looked the same and dressed the same because she was very specific about what she wanted. These sorts of calls always look like a convention of people with the same beliefs. It's scary!

How do you make yourself memorable during auditions? If you pay absolutely no attention to the casting notes, you very well might end up in a lot of trouble. You might be labeled as an actor who can't take simple directions. You might very well be asked why you didn't come to the audition dressed appropriately. Aren't you supposed to be exactly what they are looking for? Shouldn't you look like everyone else at the audition? What can you do to make yourself more memorable and still not run the risk of making the casting director angry? It takes years of experience to answer this question. Casting directors will have a major impact on your career. How you deal with them is a very delicate matter.

Each casting director has a different modus operandi. Some encourage creativity while others only encourage creativity within narrow parameters. Get to know a casting director before you go too far out on the limb. I have directed many actors in my career and have sat through many auditions. You learn a lot about auditioning when you sit on the other side of the table. Very minor differences win and lose auditions. When a casting director is involved, all the actors are good and right for the part. All the actors will read extremely well. Ninety percent of the readings will be nearly identical. This is the clone factor. It is important for the actor to do something that will create a memorability factor.

What are some things that will make you more memorable? First of all, something a lot of beginning actors forget to do is give the pre-audition interview as much importance as your audition. Put the director and producer at ease. Talk to them. Let them get to know you as a person. Establish some rapport. Let them know that you are going to be pleasant to be around and easy to get along with. Many auditions are lost in the interview when a director does not hit it off with the actor. Your personality and people skills have a huge impact on your career. It may not seem fair, but it is how the system works. Many acting schools teach courses in the art of auditioning, so take one of these courses if you can. A professional actor has to know how to make a good first impression.

Another trick that can make you more memorable is the color and style of your clothing. Give some thought to wardrobe and accessories during your auditions. Go to your audition appropriately dressed, but try to find something that will distinguish you from everyone else. For a dance call, one of my friends, Susan Gordon Clark, won an audition by wearing a red top with her leotard. Everyone else at the call wore their regular black work-out leotards because that is what they wore everyday. Everybody looked the same except Susan. She added a little bit of color to her clothes. Every dancer was pretty equal. But, Susan stood out. She was "Red Top." It was easy for everyone to pick her out. She wasn't the third dancer from the left in the sixth row. If you can gain a wardrobe advantage, use it. If you can do something with your hair to make yourself more memorable, do it. My eyebrows are very bushy; I have a bushy moustache; my glasses are distinctive. I have played up these three features to make myself more memorable.

When you are auditioning, something as simple as your name can make you more memorable than other actors. My real name is JoBe. I can't tell you how many conversations that has started in an interview. "What an unusual name! Is that your real name? Where does it come from?" When I tell them that my Father's name was Joe and my Mother's name Bea, they always remember my name. It's always easier to remember special names like Elvis, Oprah, Madonna, Cher, Pierce Brosnan, Efram Zimbalist, Jr., Mary Tyler Moore, Fabian, and Mr. T. (By the way, there is only one name available for each actor in the unions. If your name is John Doe, and there already is a John Doe in the union, you will have to create a different name for yourself to perform under. My friend Susan Gordon Clark had to add Gordon to her professional name because Susan Clark already was acting under that name. If you have to change your name, try to create a name that will stand out and be memorable.)

The gimmicks I have just talked about will sometimes give you an edge over the competition — and the difference between winning and losing is usually just a slight difference. If you have aspirations of being a professional actor, I think it is only fair to warn you about the dark side of the business of auditioning. Beware of talking to actors at auditions. Some actors will intentionally or unintentionally try to disrupt your audition to gain an advantage. This is dirty pool, but it happens. An actor will hang around after an audition and talk to the other actors about any number of subjects. The actor might mention that the producers are auditioning big stars for the role, and this audition is just a long shot so just take it as an exercise. Or the actor might say that he was all wrong for the part knowing that you are very similar to him. He might say they hate models knowing you have done a lot of modeling. Or, he might just try to engage you in conversation to take your concentration off your audition. Don't by suckered on an audition by another actor. Keep to yourself and concentrate on business. As I said, little things win and lose auditions. Don't let other actors psyche you out of a job. Hopefully you'll never experience this tactic, but if it happens to you, don't say I didn't warn you.

Lastly, what can you do as an actor to make your acting more memorable? It is really hard to out-act your peers at the highest levels. But it can be done. The more preparation time you put in, the better off you will be. Get comfortable with your part. Do it lots of ways with lots of people. Gain flexibility in your approach so you can shift approachs in an instant. A casting director will read with you. The casting director won't read it like your rehearsal partner so don't just rehearse with one person feeding you the cues. Have several people cue you so you can react to different interpretations of the cues. During the audition retain your composure. Don't be uptight. Lots of preparation time and drilling will make you more confident. Be able to improvise if necessary. In auditions, they are more interested in how you feel in the role than how perfectly you memorized the lines. Mostly importantly, try to bring something to your audition that is uniquely you. In my world, I "JoBeize it." I try to twist a line or an action that will make it unique to me. What am I talking about? In thoroughbreds, this is where class separates the winners from the losers. Every successful actor has something inside themselves that makes an audience want to watch them. Remember how I said that when stars walk into a room, everyone stops and notices that they are there? They are "the class" and their presence is not just seen, but felt. Find the part of yourself that got you to that audition, and try to bring it to the role you are auditioning for to make it unique. In *Star Wars*, Obi-Wan tells Luke to "Feel the Force! Let it flow through you." I always get goose bumps when I hear that line. My greatest advice to you is to find that part of you that is special and put it on the line. This may seem like fairly obtuse advice from a guy who analyzcs life as a series of mathematical realities and statistical charts, but it is the thing that separates the actors from the cabdrivers. Actors make magic out of motion and sound. Winning auditions means being special. Learn the basics of auditioning, prepare until no stone is unturned, give it your best shot, and never quit. It is the most any professional can do. There are no deep, mystical guarded secrets about auditioning that will win you every audition. Don't drive yourself crazy searching for them. Somebody has to win and somebody has to lose. Always do your best, and you will win your share.

CHAPTER TWENTY-NINE

I Could Have Been
a Goldfish...
(Human Resources and Safety)

Did you ever wonder what it would be like to be a goldfish, living in a little bowl? Having your own castle to swim around all day? People coming and feeding you and throwing pennies into your bowl and making wishes. That's how goldfish can afford castles, I guess. The life of a goldfish is supposed to be idyllic and peaceful. That's why the Japanese started breeding fancy goldfish hundreds of years ago. They bred the fish to have longer fins so they could swim slowly and gracefully. But goldfish exist in a perfect world. Throw them in a real lake and they become bait for the fast, ugly fish. Being an actor is sort of like being a goldfish in a bowl. People look at you because you are art; they think you are beautiful and want to lead an idyllic life like the one they see you living inside the bowl.

But the life of an actor is very different than people expect. You have to be very adaptable to an ever-changing business world around you filled with predators who will continuously put you to the test. You must learn to keep your guard up against many different obstacles that will potentially disrupt your business. Remember, actors are not employees; actors are business managers who are responsible for the success or failure of their own companies. What types of things can disrupt your idyllic life? How about something as simple as SUCCESS! At some point in everyone's career, a hot streak will occur. You will win every audition in sight. You will win all the good parts because you are IT! Suddenly, jealousy rears its ugly head and other actors will set their sights on you. They complain that you are winning too much. Agents start to suggest that actors get a haircut like yours or glasses like yours or grow a mustache like yours because that's the winning look right now. Casting directors start to ask for a (fill in your name) type. They don't want you because you are on too many things right now, and they think you're overexposed. I remember the first time this happened to me. I felt really odd. At auditions, other actors would say unsettling things to me like: "Why are you here? Aren't you making enough money?" I never expected that kind of reaction from fellow actors once I started having success. Friends you commiserated with over losing auditions feel you have progressed beyond them.

In horse racing, this means you've moved up in class. Actors sense when you have gone to another level, and many of them will treat you differently. Don't let this kind of treatment get to you. Try harder than ever to win auditions because that is the way your business will go forward. At times in my career, I backed off because I felt guilty about winning too many auditions; other actors needed work, too. In retrospect, this was unbelievably dumb. As you move up in class, you will leave some friends behind because their careers will not go forward as quickly as yours. If you have a friend that is winning everything in sight, encourage them forward to even greater successes; they will appreciate you as a friend even more. Acting is a dog-eat-dog business. When you start becoming successful, play your string of successes out as long as you can. It is the right thing for any business to do. One of the most successful announcers I know is Joel Cory. At an audition, a struggling young announcer asked him why he was auditioning for a small job. "Did he want to do everything?" Without hesitating, Joel looked at him and said: "Actually, yes. I do want to do everything. I always try to win every audition. I want to do every job that I can." That young struggling announcer felt very embarrassed. He tried to go head to head against a thoroughbred. Hopefully, he learned something. Thoroughbreds always love to win just like professional actors always love to win — that is why they have careers filled with successes instead of moments of success. Winning is always your first priority. Don't allow less successful actors to dissuade you from attempting to win auditions.

What are some other obstacles that can wreck a beautiful day? Did you ever shoot yourself in the foot? I guess a lot of cowboys used to do that because when their six-shooters were in their holsters they pointed down at their feet. As they did a fast draw to shoot a bad cowboy in a black hat, they would accidentally pull the trigger before they got the gun out of their holster and shoot themselves in the foot. Likewise, an actor can shoot his mouth off and end up shooting himself in the foot. Never think out loud. Never talk yourself out of a job. When I was doing a lot of musical theater, a producer asked me if I could sing. I was singing the comic parts in musicals. But, I thought before I answered. Trying to sound modest, I said: "Well, I can't sing like the people who do leads in musicals! Those people can really, really sing compared to me. I get by, though." The producer assumed I couldn't sing. Little did I know that he wanted me to do the voice of the Hamburger Helper Hand. I certainly could have sung well enough to do that. He hired another actor (Joel Cory) to do the job and told him: "Do it like JoBe would do it IF JoBe could sing." I shot myself in the foot. Actors find lots of ways to shoot themselves in the foot. Never talk about reasons you cannot do a job. Don't talk about vacations that might get in the way of work or other jobs that might cause schedule conflicts. All a producer will remember is that you are not available. Don't give the impression that you are so busy, you are not interested in the job. Don't give the impression that you might not be able to handle the job (like I did in the above example). In short, don't talk about anything that might give the impression that you are not going to be 100 percent available to do the work and 100 percent interested in doing the job. When you are asked if you are available and/or interested in doing the job, say: "yes." A producer and director will remember "yes." It is a simple answer. This might seem like common sense, but it is amazing how many times I have seen actors cost themselves jobs because they talked too much.

While I am on the subject, never use the pity approach. Producers like to work with successful, working actors — actors with a positive attitudes. If you go into an audition moaning and groaning about how little you've been working, it raises a red flag. Why haven't you been working? Are you a problem to work with? Are you unreliable? Will your depressed attitude affect your work? Producers will not feel sorry for you; they will avoid you like the plague. If you are ill or have had a personal tragedy in your life, don't talk about it in an audition. Don't point out the fact that you have a very bad cold and crawled off your sick bed to shake hands with the producer and director and give them the same strain of influenza that you have. Don't tell them that you just had a serious injury and question if you are capable of doing the work; if you question if you can do the work, have your agent find out the particulars before the audition and make a decision. The moment you make yourself questionable for a job is the moment you eliminate yourself from the competition for the job. Don't talk about death in auditions. If your dog just died, everyone will feel bad for you, but it will cast gloom over your audition. Don't mention it since it has nothing to do with your audition.

Why do I mention something as crazy as: Don't talk about death in auditions? I bring this up because I once had a studio sales representative that frequently fell into the trap of mentioning negative things on sales calls. I spoke to him about it frequently. Before a big presentation, I went over a list of don'ts I wanted him to avoid in the presentation. To be funny, I concluded the lecture by warning him to especially avoid talking about death or dismemberment. Everyone laughed and off we went to the presentation. When we were in the presentation, everything was going very well. The client was happy, and we were happy. The final subject of the meeting was casting. To close the deal, all we needed to do was come up with an actor who could do a wonderful job. The client talked about an actor they really loved and had used in years past. We all knew that actor had died an awful death the week before. My studio sales representative could not wait to break the news! My entire staff held its breath as we watched him mumble and fumble and try to avoid the temptation of talking about death. Believe me, the subject will come up at some point in your career; don't talk about it. Tom Sawyer and Huck Finn held their breath when they walked past a cemetery. Do the same!

Life inside the goldfish bowl can be made traumatic by outside predators, too. Every goldfish fears the family cat. A day will come when a "catty" client will see you at an audition and pick you as the goldfish they want to torment and toy with like catnip! The difficult client will drive you insane. Nothing you do is right. No actor is more perfect for the part, but you just can't do it the way they thought you would do it. For example, I was hired to do the voice of an animated cat who was writing to an advice columnist. I had three sentences to say. The first was: "Dear Kitty." I did sixty-five takes of those two words, and not one of the takes was right. The producer said none was even close. The producer gave me pages and pages of notes to explain the meaning of the line so that I could imbue it with the perfect inflection. I was told the cat's life history that drove it to write this letter that epitomized the cat's lifelong struggle and moment of *cat*harsis. The producer said the line and asked me to mimic the exact inflections. I mimicked the producer exactly, but that still wasn't it. I didn't understand the irony and nuance of "Dear Kitty." Nothing worked. I did hundreds of takes. "Dear Kitty" became a mantra and I started to loose touch with reality. Finally, the producer ended the session. The producer was not happy, but would make do with what I could deliver. A few days later, a casting call went out for the voice of The Cat. Every major voice actor was asked to audition. One unfortunate actor won the audition and experienced a fate similar to mine. A few days later, I was asked to come back and do the voice, again. The producer told me about the auditions, and how incapable and uncooperative all the other actors were compared to me. I was bad, but they were worse, so the job was mine. I was the perfect voice if I could just do the voice like the producer wanted. The producer would get it out of me if she had to do it syllable by syllable. Lucky me. They tied me down to the rack for a couple hundred tortured takes and mercifully let me go. I was nice about it, apologized for taking so long to get it, and thanked everyone very much. I made a lot of money. If you live life in a goldfish bowl, you will have days like this. My advice is to do your best and get through them. Keep your cool; once the job is over, you'll never have to work with these people again! Don't cave into the pressure and create a scene and walk out. If you do, you will always be the bad guy. Make the best of the situation. Sometimes that is all you can do. Just because they are not professional doesn't mean that you shouldn't be. Or to put it another way, life is filled with idiots, don't allow yourself to be one of them.

One of the principal sins of every actor is covetousness. No matter how well you are doing, you always want the other actor's career. You peer from your goldfish bowl across your agent's office into another goldfish bowl. That goldfish has a bigger, better castle. You make your own life miserable coveting that castle. Many actors focus a lot of their energy brooding over what hasn't happened. They spend more time thinking about almosts, if only's, and what if's than they do on "I'm gonnas." But life is not perfect. Learn to do the best you can with what you've got. Concentrate your attention on making the most of every opportunity you are given because you never know where it will lead. One time on an industrial video my supporting cast included two actors from the Organic Theater company, Joe Mantegna and Dennis Franz. Needless to say, those two actors went on to much bigger careers than mine. At the time, they weren't well-known stars, but the project worked out very well, and I'm proud of the work I did with them. So always do the best you can with what you've got. As I look back on my career, I have done many jobs with big stars before they were famous. We did commercials, industrial videos, photo shoots, or stage plays. Some people I worked with before they were stars include John Mahoney, Bill Murray, Betty Thomas, Judith Ivey, Shelley Long, John Hughes, John Malkovich, John Candy, George Wendt, Tim Kazurinsky, Tim Meadows, Tim Reid, Dan Castellaneta, Dennis Farina, and David Copperfield. I didn't work on major projects with these people, but I worked with them. I'm glad I had the opportunity, and I always gave the job my best effort. Don't make yourself crazy because life doesn't work out the way you thought it would; be thankful for what you've got. When you look back on it some day, it might be better than you think.

One last little bit of advice about life in the goldfish bowl. Life will be what you make it. You are in charge. The quality of your work will eventually determine the size of your castle and the life you lead. The jobs you attract and accept will eventually tell the tale of what you have become. Do work you are proud of. There will be times when you are offered jobs that will make you think twice about accepting them. Do you want to do nude scenes? Do you want to do open-mouth kissing scenes? (Both of these questions are covered at length with rules and regulations by Screen Actors Guild.) How would you feel about portraying a child molester? Would you want to appear as a guest on Jerry Springer or Montel Williams? As you accept questionable jobs, you have to be willing to live with the consequences. They will propel your career in one direction or another because they are considered controversial. Be careful because they might point your career down a path that you might later regret. One time I had trouble deciding if I should accept a film role. One of my recording engineers, Ralph Rocha, solved the problem for me. He asked me if I would want my children to see the film ten years from now. I knew I wouldn't, so I turned the part down. One of my friends did a horror film and couldn't sit through the screening. You have to live with what you do. So if you accept a job, do the best you can with it and make sure you can commit to giving it your all. In the case of commercials, television, and films, your work will be out there for a long time. Make sure you will be proud of it for years to come. Life in a goldfish bowl will be what you make it.

CHAPTER THIRTY

I Could Have Been a Eulogist...

(Business Axioms)

I wonder if anyone makes a full-time living as a eulogist? In any case, I bet a eulogist never has to worry about a client complaining. Who pays a eulogist? I'll have to look into this. Maybe then I can write a book called *I Could Have Been a Cabdriver. . . But I Became a Eulogist Instead.* On the other hand, maybe I won't. Eulogists always get in the last word, though, and since I'm nearing the end of the book I thought a final chapter about famous last words would be appropriate. Because my penchant to organize has got me where I am today, I needed to find a way to put down a whole series of unrelated thoughts into a useful assemblage. What follows is a series of sentences you will hear at some point in your career and what they mean.

1) **"We'll know what we're looking for, when we hear (see) it."**
    This phrase is generally used by "creative" people who

have a mediocre script and are looking for a very creative actor to save the project. The writer, director, and producer don't have any idea how to make the script work. They compensate by having an enormous casting call. They sometimes watch hundreds of actors bring their creativity to the project hoping for a good idea. The truth of the matter is they have a germ of an idea and want someone else to do their work.

2) **"Don't worry. We'll save it in editing."** This is a nice way of telling you not to expect much when you see yourself on television or at the movies. It is also a diplomatic way of telling you that the scene will be reshot with another actor.

3) **"We've almost got the money raised. We're seeing someone tomorrow."** Many theater and small film project producers use this. Don't hold your breath when they say it to you. Raising money is the most difficult part of the theater and film businesses. Novice producers always think it will be easy. But it never, ever is easy. The odds of success are much longer than the longest of long shots. Unless you are working with a producer with a long and successful track record, there is very little chance that the project will happen.

4) **"The check is in the mail."** No business ever likes to hear this phrase. It means the producer that owes you money has no money, or it means that the producer is using your money to finance his or her next project. In any case, write the money off as a loss and be pleasantly surprised if you see one dime. If you can learn to do this, I guarantee you'll live a more peaceful life.

5) **"You're perfect! Are you available? We'll call your agent as soon as we've finished the auditions."** This phrase is known as "the kiss of death." Every actor learns to dread this statement. Why producers and directors use it is beyond me. Maybe they say this to every actor to let them know they've done a good job, but it builds false expectations.

6) **"I've got it, but I just want to do one more take."** If a director says this to you, it is important to understand that he or she doesn't mean it. You will do many more takes of the same shot. The more difficult the take, the more takes you will do. Just when you think you are done, you start all over, again. This phrase signals a beginning, not an end.

7) **"Can you shave your face/legs seventy-five times a day?"** A lot of other stupid questions can be substituted for this one. I used this one because it was the first really stupid question anyone asked me. I was auditioning for a razor blade commercial. The casting director wanted to find someone whose skin could be shaved seventy-five times in a day. Who could possibly know if their skin could hold up to seventy-five shavings without getting irritated? Here are a couple of other really dumb questions. Can you run a four-minute mile? (Yeah, me and the other fifteen guys in the world that can do it are all coming in today.) Can you do sit-ups for ten hours? (With or without convulsing?) You occasionally will be asked really dumb questions. Take a moment to think before answering them. Very few people in the world could have honestly answered the above questions affirmatively. You don't want to take yourself out of the competition for these jobs because the person asking the questions speaks in hyperbole.

Remember that you are an actor. Actors can be superhuman in movies, but in real life you are flesh and bone just like everyone else. When someone asks if you can do the impossible, they probably don't mean it.

8) **"I didn't believe the reading. I don't think a real chicken would talk like that."** During your career, you will find yourself in many surreal situations. Creative directors will get very serious with you about getting into the role of a chicken or a talking sponge. But if you are drawn to acting you will probably feel comfortable devoting your life to pondering how a real chicken would talk. An actor's life is filled with bizarre moments. Enjoy them. That's entertainment.

9) **"You'll be done by noon."** If you become a popular, working actor, you'll hear this phrase from time to time. Unfortunately, it frequently leads to your getting a divorce. Here's how it works. You plan something special with your spouse. You look forward to it for months. In fact, it is such a special event that you tell your agent not to take any bookings that day. As you are getting ready to leave, a producer calls to book you on that day. He has to have you. He can't live without you. Your agent tells him you have something special planned with your spouse and are leaving town that night. The producer promises: "You'll be done by noon." You take the producer at his word and end up working until midnight. Then you get a divorce. But you do have another option. You talk your spouse into postponing your plans by one day. It costs you a lot of money to change your plans, but you make a responsible business decision to keep your client happy. As soon as you have changed your plans, the producer cancels the job. You go off on your trip in a bad mood, have a lousy

time, and return home to get a divorce. No matter what you do, you are in a no-win situation the minute a producer says: "You'll be done by noon."

10) **"The reviews were mixed."** This is what the producer says the night after a show opens and the day before he puts up the two-week closing notice. It means no matter how many times the producer read the reviews, he couldn't find a critic who wrote any phrases in a review that could be mistaken as positive comments.

11) **"We'll do lunch."** This is what a non-working actor says to a working actor in an effort to find out how the working actor is getting work. Usually, the working actor cancels lunch at the last minute because of an unexpected job which irritates the non-working actor even more.

12) **"Put him on ice."** This phrase can be good or bad. The term *ice* means that a producer is putting an actor on hold for a day in the future; he has right of first refusal if you get another job offer. One date is a good sign. If the producer asks for six dates for a one-day job, the production is shaky. The client may not want to do the shoot, there many be financial or legal problems, they may have another actor waiting in the wings. As you go on other auditions, don't tell them you are on ice for six days for a one-day job. It is just like saying you are not available. Take care of your business first. When decision time comes, let your agent deal with the producers.

13) **"What do you really do for a living?"** You'll hear this a lot. Once you get to be a working professional, it feels really great to be able to smile back and respond: "I'm a professional actor; I don't have time to do anything else."

People always assume that actors have to do something else to make money so they can live their Bohemian lives. When people find out you're actually earning a full-time living as an actor, they usually stand stunned in disbelief before they say: "Wow!. . . really?" Their whole perception of you will then change forever. You are a real actor, and they had a chance to meet you.

CHAPTER THIRTY-ONE

I Could Have Been an Actor...

(Afterword)

I like this last title. I actually became an actor. I did what I set out to do. I'm not a star. But, I spent the last thirty years in the business. I never had to take a menial job to support myself, and I have only collected two weeks of unemployment during my entire career. (AFTRA and SAG were on strike for an extended period, and I couldn't find a part in a stage play.) I always figured out a way to keep going because I operated my career as a business. In this book I have tried to pass along the ways I did it. I have also tried to give you a feeling of what it is like to be a work-a-day actor. I have a few Hollywood credits, but they are modest ones. I've done some nice theater work, but it hasn't been Broadway. My biggest successes have been in commercials and industrial videos. Since I chose to live my life in Chicago, those were the biggest opportunities I was able to get with regularity. I'm proud of what I've accomplished. I've done the best I could with the opportunities I had.

I've managed to have a full-time career as an actor for over thirty years. Not only did I have a career, but I have a wife, two sons, a house, a vacation house, insurance, savings, investments, my own recording studios, and a very nice retirement fund — just like somebody who has a real job! So take heart, it can be done. I've had more than my share of days in the sun, and they've been wonderful. But most of my time has been spent doing the day-to-day acting jobs like commercials and industrial films. I've been good enough to stay in the business and pay the bills for my family. I've included my acting résumé at the end of the book. It is a list of the highlights of my career over the past thirty years. When you read over my résumé, I think you'll get a feeling of the kind and number of successes you can reasonably expect to have if you have a career like mine. When you realize that they can all be included on one page, it might not seem like much, but it was more than enough to keep me going. When I wrote my first résumé, I wondered how I would be able to fill a single page. Now, when look at my résumé, I realize I have enough experiences to fill an entire book!

I hope my book helps you become a professional actor. Since I plan on working another thirty years, I hope we'll have a chance to work together some day.

Break a leg!

JOBE CERNY   **STEWART TALENT**-Chicago (312) 943-3131
SAG, AFTRA, AEA   Height 5'7" Weight 200

FILM
ROAD TO PERDITION, Dreamworks, d/Sam Mendes
NOVOCAINE, Artisan Entertainment, d/David Atkins
UNCONDITIONAL LOVE, New Line Cinema, d/P.J. Hogan
LOVE AND ACTION, L&A Productions, d/Dwayne Johnson-Cochran
MY BEST FRIEND'S WEDDING, Tri-Star Pictures, d/P.J. Hogan
MO MONEY, Columbia Pictures d/Peter McDonald
PRELUDE TO A KISS, 20th Century Fox, d/Norman Rene
DREAMER, 20th Century Fox, d/Noel Nosseck
RENT-A-COP, Bon-Bon International, d/Thebus/Coch
CONTINENTAL DIVIDE, Universal, d/Michael Apted
SOMEWHERE IN TIME, Universal, d/Jeannot Szwarc
DUMMY, Warner Communications
TOUGHEST MAN IN THE WORLD, CBS/Centerpoint Prod., d/Dick Lowry
IN THE NET, Dreambuilder, d/Jim Friedman & Brad Pruitt
HOTEL SOAP, Hammerhead Films, d/LeRoy Koetz
GOING HOME, Skymaster Productions, d/Tyson Lutz
PATRONIZED, Flip Films, d/Alan Lieb

EPISODIC
CHICAGO HOPE, Agent Greenblatt(Guest Star), 20th Century Fox, d/Stephen Cragg
EARLY EDITION, Conner, Columbia Pictures, d/Stephen Cragg
THE UNTOUCHABLES, Francois, Capone's Chef, Paramount, d/Colin Bucksey
LADY BLUE, John, MGM
JACK & MIKE, MGM
HOMETOWN (Pilot), The Host (Starring), d/Ken Kahle
CHICAGO STORY, The Baron, MGM (Pilot & Episode)

TELEVISION SPECIALS
OPRAH (Comedy Bit with Tim Allen)
T.V.'S COMMERCIALS, BLOOPERS, Carson/NBC
50 GREATEST COMMERCIALS OF ALL TIME, Nickelodeon
RAP MUSIC SPECIAL, MTV Special
MISTLETOE BEAR'S CHRISTMAS, 3 WGN Specials, Uncle Mistletoe

THEATER	(*indicates original production cast)	
Drury Lane	PLAY IT AGAIN SAM (Starring)	Allan Felix
Café Voltaire	*REPETE WITH MADELINE	Repete
Drury Lane	THE MAN WHO CAME TO DINNER	Banjo
Ivanhoe	*FUNERAL MARCH FOR A ONE MAN BAND	Dad/Chrisolde
Drury Lane	THE FANTASTICS	Bellomy
First Chicago	*THE MAGIC MAN	Pinchbeck
First Chicago	MIDSUMMER NIGHT'S DREAM	Flute
Drury Lane	THE ODD COUPLE	Roy
Pheasant Run	WAIT UNTIL DARK	Carlino
Willow Playhouse	SCUBA DUBA	Schoenfeld
Bridge VU	STAR-SPANGLED GIRL	Norman Cornell
Theatre	DONT DRINK THE WATER	Walter
	OH DAD, POOR DAD	Johnathan
	THE ODD COUPLE	Vinnie
	CABARET	Ernst Ludwig
	A DELICATE BALANCE	Harry

IMPROVISATION
The Second City National Touring Company, The Reification Company, The Blue Moon Players
EDUCATION B.A. Speech & Drama, Valparaiso University, M.A. Theater, Northwestern University
SPECIAL SKILLS JoBe Cerny is best known as the voice of The Pillsbury Doughboy and, on camera,
as Procter & Gamble's silent spokesman, The Cheer Man.

JoBe Cerny

STEWART
T A L E N T
58 West Huron Chicago, IL 60610
tel. 312.943.3131   fax. 312.943.5107